Playing Cards in a Hurricane

Tales of a mad and downright
dangerous voyage across the Atlantic
Ocean in a 35' yacht

Robert Oliver

Dedicated to:

Janey Hewitt, Kate Davies and Neil Shaw

for their inspiration & support and without whom, this book
would have taken another 40 years to publish !

Contents

Chapter One

The Chislehurst Plot

He used often to say that there was only one
Road; that it was like a great river: its springs were
at every doorstep and every path was its tributary.
"It's a dangerous business... going out of your
front door", he used to say. "You step into the
Road, and if you don't keep your feet, there is no
knowing where you might be swept off to".

J.R.R.Tolkien

It must be said that if anyone setting out on an adventure knew the full extent of the risks that they were about to take, mountains would be left unclimbed, oceans uncharted, skies unflown, paths unwalked, continents undiscovered. We set out in cheerful willingness, not wanting to think of the dangers ahead in case we fail before we even start. I was no different. Each of us must learn this lesson the hard way.

It was February 1983 and I was living in a public house that my parents ran in Powick, Worcester. The Red Lion was a typical old English country inn, dating back to the 17th century, nestling on a small hill overlooking the River Severn. The expanse of fields between the inn and the river was the site of the Battle of Worcester in 1651, the last battle fought on English soil. On that day, the inn was pressed into service as the field hospital. The maimed and dying were brought up from the battlefield below, perhaps giving rise to the rumoured hauntings and ghostly sightings that still surround the old inn to this day.

At that time in winter, the Red Lion was an isolated and lonely place. The lightest of snow cut off the small community from the outside world, the roads treacherous and barely passable. Nevertheless, a dogged bunch of customers would trudge through the snow on foot every evening for a quiet drink; the inn offered warmth and cheer to the few and in turn, that local trade kept the pub alive in winter.

Like them, I was trapped in the village that evening. I dared not venture out on the roads, as the only exit from the pub was a steep downward lane, now covered in sheet ice. There would be no chance of me bringing my car to a halt when I reached the main road below.

I had been unemployed for months, having resigned from my job as a computer operator late the previous year, to help my parents renovate this old pub and then ostensibly to travel but with no money or even a plan to make this happen.

That night, I was propping up the bar with a pint of real ale in my hand; a typical 22-year old with good qualifications, plenty of ambition and a thirst for life, yet thoroughly demoralised and dispirited. I could see no prospect of things changing for the better. I did not want a career in the pub trade. I did not want to go back to a repetitive job in computers. I did not want to be in Worcester anymore but I had no idea what to do about it. Many days had been spent with a paintbrush in hand. Nights had been passing slowly, always out drinking beer with friends, often playing pool. Nothing was particularly right or wrong but I knew that I was coasting along and wasting time.

My father was a gregarious, well-liked host and he drew a crowd of loyal regular customers most evenings. One of them was John, a Londoner who had ended up in Worcester - a colourful businessman that I didn't know particularly well but we fell into conversation that evening.

"I sell cars. I rent out my flats. I'm involved in a few deals here and there. Most of them proper ! I'm a quarter of a millionaire, you know ?" he said to impress me.

I'd heard that phrase a few times recently when people were trying to brag and it always cracked me up. I wondered which part of the millionaire he was tonight ? Saying "I've got a quarter of a million in the bank" would have sounded less of a small-town thing to say but I remained respectful. He might be a cartoon Cockney but he had a certain notoriety, having been to prison for money laundering. Also, it was rumoured that he had been a bit player in the Roberto Calvi[1] affair, so I was not inclined to try my luck with my normal brand of offbeat humour.

---

1. Roberto Calvi was the chairman of Banco Ambrosiana when it collapsed in 1982 amidst a $1.5 billion corruption scandal that, it was speculated, involved the Vatican Bank (IOR), the Italian mafia and the clandestine Propaganda Due masonic organisation. He disappeared in Rome and was soon discovered dead, hanging beneath Blackfriars Bridge in central London with his pockets weighted with bricks (which did not have his fingerprints on them) and $14,000 in cash.

"So what you doing, Rob ?" he asked me at last. "You seem a bright lad but you're not working at the moment, are you ?"

I explained about my several false starts: art school drop-out, failed toolmaker's apprentice, jewellery finisher, musician, supermarket manager, computer operator.

"What I really need is to get out of Worcester, go and do some travelling, see some places", I said casually.

At this remark, he paused, put down his glass and turned to me slowly, seeing me as if for the first time. His clear, inquisitive, piercing blue eyes and swept back grey hair (and despite his age), his quiet strength and nature gave me a true measure of John's presence and I was suddenly daunted.

"Do you mean that ?" he said quietly and firmly.

"Yes", I stammered.

"No, I mean do you really mean that ?"

"Yes, really I do. I wouldn't say it if I didn't." I managed.

"OK" said John. "I will give you a phone number of an old friend of mine who lives down in Portsmouth and delivers sailing yachts all over the world for people. He is always short of good crew. You just promise me that you won't waste his time, OK ? Don't use the number unless you're serious, got it ?"

I took the number and thanked him sincerely.

"Well, good luck, young man" said John with a smile at last. "Let me know how you get on".

I felt that I had been judged and got the strong sense that he knew how I would decide, although I had no idea myself.

For several days, I kept pulling the increasingly-crumpled scrap of paper out of the pocket of my jeans with the number pencilled on it, looking at it and then putting it away again. I felt that to ring the number would start a sequence of events that I would not be able to stop. I broached the subject with my parents and we discussed it several times. I could tell that they were fearful but at the same time, they knew that it could be good for me to go out and do this.

In the end, I steeled myself, dialled the Portsmouth number and got to speak to the mysterious captain, Peter "Stokie" Newington who, unusually, was at home between yacht deliveries. I introduced myself, explained about my conversation with John and offered my services.

"Stokie, I've never been on a yacht and have absolutely no experience but I really want to travel, I'm fit, I work hard and I am 100% reliable".

"That's good", he replied. "But I've got to tell you that it's very hard work. It's risky and it's dangerous at times - but the trick is not to take excessive risks. I learned to sail in the Army when I was stationed in Kiel in northern Germany ten years back so I'm formally trained and I've got my skipper's ticket. Every minute of the day that I'm sailing a yacht, I'm thinking about what might go wrong and how I can handle it. All down to experience, y'see? But don't let that put you off. You'll be safe with me and you'll have the time of your life. I'll expect you to work hard and follow orders immediately, without question. We have to have that discipline because our lives will depend on it. But it'll be a fantastic experience and you'll see places that you could never afford to go to, if you had to pay for it yourself. You realise that I can't afford to pay you, don't you? The profit margins are way too thin but all your food and travel expenses will be covered."

He paused for a moment.

"Look, my next assignment is to fly out to the States, collect a yacht from Tortola over in the British Virgin Isles (that's the Caribbean), then we cross the North Atlantic then sail through the Mediterranean to our destination, Corfu in Greece, where we drop the boat off and then fly home. It will probably take about 6 weeks and there will be a crew of three, that's me and my mate Scouse who's really good and we're looking for another."

"What do you think ? Are you up for it ? 'Cause we're leaving in three weeks !"

What - the chance to travel the world at someone else's expense and escape from Worcester in wintertime?

"I'm your man !", I blurted out without a moment's hesitation.

So, all was settled then.

The following week, I made an overnight trip to London, first to obtain a US visa from the embassy in Grosvenor Square which took several hours and from there, on to Chislehurst in south London to stay with David Blackwell, who was also a very experienced ocean sailor and ran a yacht delivery company himself. In effect, he would be sub-contracting this particular job to Stokie.

After getting thoroughly lost on the rail network in south-east London, I finally found David's cottage in Chislehurst. I was very late which immediately put me on the back foot. He was everyone's idea of an ex-Para: a tall, broad, tough looking man of action but few words. I was worried that I might let people down and doubted that he would feel comfortable putting his trust in a novice, especially for a lengthy passage across the

Atlantic and through the Mediterranean. Over dinner, I was open with him about my lack of experience and questioned my suitability for the trip but he was immensely reassuring. He explained how he had started his sailing experience in exactly the same way, starting a long sea voyage with no prior experience whatsoever. The key to success was to start under an experienced skipper and work hard, follow orders and "learn the ropes" as fast as possible.

We got on well and I returned to Worcester on the train from Paddington the next afternoon, lighter in spirit, feeling relieved that I had gained his support.

Two weeks later, on Sunday 27th February, it was time to depart. I hugged my parents and my younger brothers on the doorstep of the inn. Beneath their smiles, I could sense real apprehension and doubt but we all put on a brave face and I trudged down the drive with my rucksack on my back, waving cheerily as I left.

"Don't you worry about me. See you in six weeks !".

I retraced my train journey back to Chislehurst that afternoon and found my way easily, with no unplanned diversions this time. My confidence was growing and I felt exhilarated by the forthcoming adventure.

I was first to arrive at David's cottage. Stokie arrived next and I was pleased to finally meet the man that I was putting my life in the hands of. Like me, he was of average height, medium build but he certainly looked more the part that I did. He had a mop of curly fair hair and a Mexican Zapata moustache to match it. I could sense his military bearing and that added to his credibility. He looked like a yachtsman too – jeans, deck shoes, warm fleece and thoroughly windswept, even though we were standing in the front room of a cosy cottage.

"Good to meet you at last Rob" he said with a broad grin, "Always good to get fresh meat !"

I liked him immediately as he was exactly what I had expected – someone with the gravitas and confidence that suggested that he knew his stuff but yet with a real sense of humour too.

Finally, there was a brisk, playful rap on the door and in walked Paul Carswell, the long-awaited third man and a bundle of energy. The first thing I noticed was the easy smile, exuberance and his strong Liverpudlian accent. From that moment, as he introduced himself, I knew him only as "Scouse". A six-footer with a mop of dark, slightly thinning hair. A handsome and welcoming chap. Again, I knew that the pair of us would get on, so I was hugely relieved. I'd met my crew, felt that we could work well together and even better, they were clearly very competent and experienced, which was a huge relief.

PLAYING CARDS IN A HURRICANE

Around 8pm, David brought out bottled beers for us and the atmosphere changed, becoming serious, like a low-level military planning session. The large round dining table was cleared completely and under the low central lamp, a huge nautical chart of the North Atlantic was unrolled and stretched out. Then, another equally large chart of the Mediterranean was slid slightly underneath to overlap it and complete our route. These were objects of beauty to me: their meridians, their vertical and horizontal lines for latitude and longitude, the colourful land masses, but most impressively, the expanses of oceans that were laid bare. There was a lot of nearly-empty white space right in the middle of the table that we were poring over carefully. David and Stokie begin an earnest debate about the optimal sea routes from the Caribbean across the North Atlantic, based on the time of year, the ocean currents and likely weather. However, this didn't take long. There was no argument and the legs of a proposed route were drawn with rule and pencil with great precision by Stokie. With the route decided, the conversation turned to logistics: travel plans, which parts that the yacht were known to be missing (including the life raft) and what we were shipping by air freight or would take with us, dock yard fees, payments and people to contact. I followed the conversation but much of the detail was lost on me. I listened entranced as if I had been privileged to enter some secret guild - the terminology and the atmosphere in the room seemed both arcane and purposeful at the same time.

Within three hours, the conversation was spent and the plans were laid. The maps were rolled up and put away by David, we checked our kit and made our final preparations for the morning and retired to our rooms.

I lay in bed thinking that I was only hours away from my biggest adventure, quietly excited and pleased that I had signed up for it. The next day, we were taking the underground to Heathrow airport to catch our Pan Am flight to Miami, Florida.

Chapter Two

Precarious

Our flight to Miami was routine enough, if being crammed into economy class with 300 other souls on a Pan Am jumbo jet could be considered routine. I loved flying but the appeal of this particular journey soon paled. In 1983, "in-flight entertainment" had not been invented, so there was no multimedia feast of film channels, video games and music. I ate, slept, read and listened to my new Sony Walkman, of which I was immensely proud and managed to shut out the noise and increasing squalor of this long-haul flight.

After some 10 hours, we touched down in Miami and emerged blinking from the aircraft into the blazing bright warmth of a Florida afternoon. Next, we sampled the dubious delights of US Immigration which even to my young years, appeared bizarrely self-important and clearly in need of a visit to charm school. When I reached the front of the queue, I made the simple mistake of putting the tip of my right shoe over the white line and was sent to the back of the queue like a naughty child, delaying our little group somewhat.

Our two connecting flights to Tortola were not scheduled until the next day, so we decided to take in the sights. Having seen enough episodes of Miami Vice to educate us, we had come to expect that a trip into the city would be taken as an invitation to be drugged, robbed and shot so we asked a taxi driver about the famous beach instead: "Yeah, it's plenty safe enough. Just as long as you're off the streets by dark."

So, to save money, we took a long, silver bus from the airport to the beach. It was amazing how just one short bus journey could give you such an excellent insight into the American Way. Our adventure seemed to start immediately. As a polite Englishman, Stokie offered his seat to a rather elegant, elderly lady. She was so surprised and grateful that we all suspected that, either she had never been offered a seat on a bus before or never met an Englishman, or perhaps both. She was so grateful in fact, that she felt duty bound to tell us her life story. "You know, in the thirties, I used to play baseball with Babe Ruth ! Yah ever heard a' him boys ? I used to love playing baseball, those men were so virile, they had such cute 'lil bodies !". Eventually, she subsided and we stood strap-hanging for a few minutes, watching as the bus took us closer to the tall, gleaming white apartment blocks of the Beach that we had seen so many times on the television. Although none of had been here before, the skyline was so recognisable that we all confessed to feelings of déjà vu.

The bus paused and a handsome, well-dressed, young black guy boarded. He stood in front of our only exit, strap-hanging like us. He paused dramatically for breath, taking a moment to scan the faces of his audience before he launched: "You are all headed for hell and damnation. You gonna burn in fire and brimstone for your sins. Turn to Jesus. Shame the Devil" and so it went. As good Englishman, we gave him our embarrassed half-attention, not knowing where to look whilst his seated American audience ignored him to a man.

To our immense relief, our stop arrived, we edged past the preacher and fell out onto the sidewalk, cackling with embarrassment and disbelief as the bus pulled away.

Having arrived at the famous beach, we were instantly lost and so Stokie turned to a beautiful, young lady and asked for directions. She was very happy to oblige and as she talked, my gaze turned downwards to the animal she was walking on a red leather lead. "My God, you're walking a big white cat! I've never seen that before", I blurted out. "Oh yeah" she said with a smile, "I do it to save her from the Toms around here". So even the cats were dangerous in Miami, I thought to myself.

As we walked, we were still reeling from the encounters with the oversexed baseball widow, the "hell and damnation" preacher and the cat-walking beauty but we laughed at that exhilarating madness of it all.

Finally, we were standing on a tropical beach that stretched as far as the eye could see, with beautiful fine sand between our toes, in time for the most spectacular sunset. Most importantly for me, it was February 28th and I had escaped from the winter cold of Powick, Worcestershire. Scouse was not impressed, "More like bleedin' Butlins", said he.

Mindful of the taxi driver's warning, we headed back to the airport and spent an uncomfortable and fitful night sleeping rough on the carpeted floor of an immense lounge, whilst cleaning machines the size of golf buggies traced around us at regular intervals. Nothing but the best for Stokie's elite crew.

Mid-afternoon, our shuttle flight departed for San Juan in Puerto Rico, the next leg of our journey. This take-off ranked as one of the worst of my life, as no more than one minute into the flight, the large jet banked viciously to the left and the pilot applied full power. "There was another plane down there - I saw it !", exclaimed Stokie. Our vacation in Puerto Rico was limited to a ten-minute dash through the airport to the British Virgin Islands airline terminal. As we rushed through the narrow corridors in the tropical heat, I joked that we were about to find a war-time Dakota waiting for us as our next flight. Sure enough, as we reached the counter breathlessly and looked out of the window, The Joke was indeed standing patiently outside the terminal building for us to board.

Secretly, I was very excited by this. Flying had always fascinated me and the chance to go up in one of those ancient propeller planes was rare indeed. Seated near the front, the three of us were in a prime position to watch the take-off through the open cockpit door. The cabin interior and the flight controls looked so antiquated and the speed of the old plane was so horrifically slow to this child of the jet age. Gradually, we edged out over the Caribbean, trying to identify the lush green islands that passed beneath us. From my window seat, I watched as a small, thin vapour trail of aviation fuel leaked from a small round blister panel on top of the port engine but I said nothing. Eventually, we turned towards one of the islands and landed smoothly on Beef Island. Tortola had no airport but was linked to the smaller island by a road bridge.

The next hour gave us our first taste of Tortola efficiency, courtesy of BVI airlines. They had delivered us safely along with our personal kitbags but the sail bag containing the Radio Direction

Finder, the Atlantic charts and the boat spares had gone missing. We couldn't set sail without any of them. We waited at the airport in vain until dusk and then took a taxi to Nanny Cay, the settlement and dockyard where the yacht was lying.

Despite being told that the yacht was ready to sail and already in the water, we had been harbouring the suspicion that all was not well. Sure enough, after searching the marina and its boatyard with a helpful guard by torchlight, we found our boat propped up on stilts high above the concrete. We found that she was indeed a Swedish-built Maxi yacht, 35 feet in length, named "Kezia of Tortola", so at least that information was correct.

My initial impression, albeit in the darkness, suggested that she was fit for the task in hand, ruggedly handsome, robust and spacious. We climbed the ladder, dumped our kitbags and settled down for our first night on board, six feet up in the air.

The next morning, boatyard riggers finished painting the hull and when this had dried, a mobile dock crane arrived to lift the yacht into the water. By then, realisation was dawning on us that the boat was far from ready to go to sea. In fact, in daylight, we could see that it had been repeatedly cannibalised for fittings and equipment over a long period to keep other yachts in its flotilla serviceable. We inspected the big Volvo Penta engine that lived under the sealed compartment that also served as a table in the saloon and declared it to be "tired". The log that measured speed and nautical miles, much like a car speedometer, was not connected. The compass, normally filled with alcohol, was half-empty and had no light for sailing at night. The yacht's batteries were flat and had to be removed and recharged. All over the boat, many of the galvanised metal fittings were corroding.

However, all these were minor problems that were within our power to fix reasonably quickly but they were nothing compared to the dilemma caused by BVI airlines. Not only had they misplaced a vital piece of baggage but they had also misplaced the life-raft that was shipped over from England, three weeks ago.

These issues would be irritating to resolve in England but in Tortola, they had the potential to become "show-stoppers" – no voyage. Dealing with local officials proved to be exasperating – we found that they could be polite, warm and helpful or completely disinterested, half-hearted or downright lazy. It took repeated, fruitless phone calls and continuous nagging to get even the smallest tasks completed when there was so much to be done to make the yacht ready for an ocean-going passage. We were being frustrated at every turn.

In all fairness to the good people of Tortola, I understood that they had different priorities. We were in a foreign country trying to fit in with their pace of life and their values.

This was never clearer to us than in the evenings. When the intense heat died down, the locals emerged and the music of steel drums wafted across the balmy air. Unfortunately, we didn't have much opportunity to enjoy the night life – we were on a very tight budget and the price of drinks (except for local rum) made it impossible. A small can of Budweiser was well over £1 which in 1983 was a small fortune. However, we sat nearby and enjoyed the lilting, cheerful music and I found the atmosphere of Tortola intoxicating in itself. I was still revelling in the fact that this country boy had escaped an English winter and found himself in the Caribbean.

The whole island was a delight. Lush greenery, tropical heat and glassy turquoise seas were all wonderful to me. The roads were populated only with older American cars – it seemed paradoxical that they were all left-hand drives but driving on the left, as in Britain.

As our preparations continued, we settled into a daily routine . Not only were we replacing broken and worn parts, cleaning and painting but Scouse took time every day to teach me what I needed to know as a crewman in the weeks ahead. I learned about the yacht's equipment, sail handling and most of all, how to tie knots. I become adept at bowlines, reef, stop-knots and figure-of-eights and practiced continuously, knowing that I needed to be able to tie them in the dark, cold and wet, while the deck of the boat tossed up and down. If only I had known why and when to use each knot....

One morning, Stokie volunteered me for the task of being hoisted up the main mast to the very top in order to check and tighten the VHF radio aerial. This involved sitting in a bosun's chair (basically a seat made from a single piece of wood) attached to the main rope (or "sheet") that normally hoists the mainsail. Stokie and Scouse attached the other end of the rope to a winch and they hand-cranked this in turns. With no head for heights, this became silent torture for me because as I was winched towards the top, the yacht began to sway violently from side to side due to the tidal swell in the marina. It felt as if I would be pitched out of my seat and fall down onto the deck some 20 feet below. Despite my fear, I said nothing as I had realised (correctly as it turned out) that this was really a trial to test my mettle and courage. Once at the top, I managed to tighten up the aerial and was winched back down to approving nods from the other two. Only when I was safely down did they point out that the rope they had winched me up on was badly-frayed but this hadn't been apparent to any of us at the start, which they found highly amusing. I managed a wry smile – this boat seemed to be sharpening our gallows humour.

As we settled into our routine, Scouse and I stopped work on the yacht each day around noon and walked to the furthest wooden pontoon facing the sea and cooled our mosquito-bitten feet in the water. Pelicans provided our entertainment, struggling in an ungainly fashion to a decent height and on spying a barracuda basking in the shallows, folded their wings and dropped like a stone, disappearing from view in a splash of foam. At the beginning, we liked to pass the time of day with the almost exclusive American population in the marina but we tired of hearing the same stories.

The US yacht skippers compared notes amongst themselves on the dangers of their passage to Tortola and for several days, we assumed that they were talking about the North Atlantic because of their hair-raising, life-threatening stories. When it dawned on us that they were talking about their short journey down from Florida, we lost all respect for them in the light of what we were about to do. When they heard of our little expedition to Corfu, their unanimous verdict was "That's suicide !" so we joined in the banter and wrote them off as "day trippers from Florida" !

We revelled in playing the part of English eccentrics. Scouse and I dressed in blue and white chequered chef's trousers because they were thinner and cooler than normal jeans and dried more quickly – but we looked like catering staff that had recently escaped from a restaurant which both amused and confused everyone else.

PLAYING CARDS IN A HURRICANE

By then, it was Wednesday and a Royal Navy cruiser, HMS Zulu sailed into Roadtown Bay and dropped anchor. Stokie found the bursar was an old friend, who plied him with drink and most usefully for us, spares that included shackles, spare lines, dozens of torch batteries and fluorescent night-lights which later, we put to good use during storms in the North Atlantic.

Slowly, Kezia was becoming more seaworthy. Scouse rang the airline to see if they had traced the sail bag containing the key equipment:

"Yeah man, it's here".

"Well, could you put it in a taxi and send it down to us ?"

"No, can't do that man".

"Why not ?"

"Too busy with the planes". Click.

Wearily, Scouse took a taxi out to the airport on Beef Island and found the bag at the foot of the gentleman's desk with the taxi rank just outside his window. Aircraft were rushing in at the rate of three every day.

Sitting at the table in the marina bar with Stokie at 10 o'clock that morning, he decided to order breakfast. For himself. Having not eaten in two days and being extremely hungry, this was too much for me to stomach and I decided to walk along the marina to rid myself of the smell of his bacon and eggs. When I collared him later about this, he said that he "did not feel responsible for onshore expenses". Clearly, he had failed to grasp that if the yacht had been sea-worthy, we would be underway by now and enjoying "offshore" conditions - including food for his crew to eat.

By the following Tuesday, we had both the missing bag and the life-raft. Getting ready to sail, we headed to a local supermarket and provisioned the yacht for the trip for a total of US$ 180, under Stokie's watchful eye. This assumed that our next stop would be in Spain or Portugal. By necessity, much of this food had to be tinned to keep for a month, although we had a reasonable stock of perishables including potatoes, fresh fruit and vegetables, knowing full well that this would last only for the first week. The advent of dehydrated "add water" ready meals had barely started in 1983 and were way beyond our means. However, Scouse used his chef's experience to buy herbs and spices that would continue to work wonders on our umpteenth meal of tinned mince and boiled rice in the weeks to come.

It had to be said that the weather was not perfect and Stokie paced the beaches, looking anxiously at the sea and the sky. We were waiting for The Right Moment.

And finally, it came on Wednesday 9th March at 7.45am. We slipped our mooring at Nanny Cay and headed out into the 2,400 empty miles of the North Atlantic.

Chapter Three

Unchained

Day 1 – Wednesday 9th March 1983:

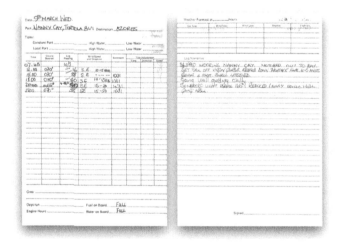

Within five minutes, I was wondering if the boat was capable of the task ahead. Motoring into the sea, the bow of the yacht buried itself into each successive wave and we were all immediately soaked. Not an encouraging start. Later on, we admitted that each of us was quietly thinking of turning back at this moment but couldn't bear to appear cowardly and so we each stayed quiet. Besides, going back to a chorus of "I told you so" from the Americans would have been too much to bear.

Stokie, by custom, took the first watch and we motored out into the ocean. At midday, we put up a small amount of jib sail as we passed the island of Virgin Gorda – the Fat Virgin – and the ploughing motion ceased. We were very cautious in our handling of the yacht in those first hours until we felt confident in her, hence the small amount of sail.

Sitting at the helm for the first time, I was absorbed by the expanse of ocean ahead and the enormity and risk of what we were taking on, was coming home to me. I was given a compass point to steer to and I focused intently on keeping the yacht on that course as best I could. I could sense the powerful flow of the water under the yacht, transmitting from the rudder and up to the large wheel in my hands. I made small instinctive movements to keep us on course, trying not to jerk or over-correct as I steered.

"You're a natural!" exclaimed Stokie. "You look like you've been doing that for years!"

I was both proud and pleased. I knew I could do this and do it well. Steering a yacht well was a combination of watchful attention and dexterity. I was aware of the responsibility for the yacht and looked around constantly for any risks or dangers, yet it was strangely relaxing at the same time.

Stokie began a tour guide routine, singling out one island as the infamous Dead Chest Island. It looked like an ordinary piece of rock but the thought that we were plying the sea routes of the 18th century pirates was not lost on any of us.

We settled quickly into the routine of keeping watch. With such a small crew, we rotated through a sequence of three hours on duty during the day and six hours off, and then at night, two hours on and four hours off because of the continual strain in concentrating in the darkness and watching for ships (which were always going to be bigger than us).

It must be said that the keeping watch to this schedule for weeks, drove each of us to the point of exhaustion before we saw land again. In theory, at least six hours off should give reasonable time to rest but in practice, the occasional but urgent sailing activity such as changing and adjusting sails, plus cooking duties, meant that we rarely achieved it.

Unfortunately, we had no self-steering gear either (although widely available in 1983) which meant that every single mile of our journey had be steered with a human hand on the tiller.

"Rob, you get your head down for a few hours", said Stokie at last, "I'll gave you a call at midnight for your first night watch".

So, I headed for my new cabin in the bows and quickly stripped to my underwear because the ploughing motion of the yacht made me feel queasy whenever I stood upright below deck. I slid into my sleeping bag as fast as I could manage. The mild nausea faded quickly now that I was lying flat. Stretched out on the luxurious expanse that was my new bed, I felt warm and comfortable although I could feel that I was sunburned from all the hours spent on deck. Within minutes, I was fast asleep after the exertions of the day.

An hour later, I was shocked awake by a dull blow to the head and I knew instantly that I had been up on the cabin ceiling which was only 4 feet above my head anyway. Realising that this was due only to the yacht pitching up and down the waves, as it had been doing all day long, I rolled over and went back to sleep. The second blow was irritating. Once I had achieved temporary weightlessness for the fifth time, I realised that I would never be able to sleep here in this wonderful, luxuriously-large cabin. Being wide awake now, I got dressed and headed through the cabin and back up onto the deck.

"There's no way I can sleep in there", I shouted across to the others, "I've been up on the ceiling five times and I'm very hacked off."

"Well you chose that berth, mate !" said Scouse.

"Yeah but I've literally been smacking my head on the roof".

By this time, Stokie and Scouse were laughing out loud at me and I was starting to realise that they had been playing me all along. Stokie took pity on me, sidling over to where I was slumped in the cockpit and put a friendly hand on my shoulder.

"You haven't got it yet, have you?"

"No ! C'mon then, put me out of my misery. Explain it to me".

"Any sailing vessel cuts through the waves bows first. Think of a boat being like a hinge. The hinge itself is at the very back of the boat, so that part only travels up and down to a very small degree whereas the bows of the boat can travel up and down by several meters. That is why the captain (that is me by the way) always has first dibs on the rear cabin and leaves everyone else to fight it out. I suggest that you take the berth across from Scouse, you might avoid a fractured skull that way!"

I was laughing at my own naivety and stupidity as well now – it was obvious enough if you knew your Physics. Unfortunately, that had been one of only two subjects that I had failed miserably at 'O' level – I should have paid more attention in class.

I went back down below and moved all my belongings to the spare berth in the main saloon and that became my 'home from home' for the rest of our time together.

Day 2 - Thursday 10th March:

That day proved to be by far the toughest of the entire voyage for me personally, which was unfortunate as it was my 23rd birthday. I had spent all the previous day on deck as it eased the sea sickness that I was suffering but in the very pleasant cooling breeze without a T-shirt, I hadn't noticed that sunstroke was setting in nor that my back, chest and shoulders were badly burned. A second-degree continuous, blistered burn across my shoulder that was splashed continuously with salt water was bad enough, without the compounding misery of sea sickness. Scouse roused my flagging spirits with a strange concoction of stew and tinned peas. Too strange, regrettably, for my weak stomach.

At 7pm, Stokie took his first sextant sighting on the setting sun in order to fix our position. I watched with fascination as he brought out this instrument from its wooden box. Even in 1983, it seemed so old-fashioned and arcane, with its brass fittings, triangular shape and small telescope sight attached. Once he had lined this up with the sun (and it had special, round, ultraviolet filters that swung into place to protect one's eyesight), he looked at the calibrations on the side of the sextant that gave him a measurement, in this case 39°26'.6 and as his eager apprentice, sitting by his side, I wrote this into the red hardback ship's log in which we recorded our progress formally, up to 10 times every day.

Next, he looked to his elegant gold watched to fix the time too. "Damn !", he shouted, "it's bloody well stopped!" He looked panic-stricken – a sextant sighting without a precise time to accompany it was absolutely useless but then he looked to my wrist. In preparing for this trip, I had decided not to bring the beautiful Montine that my parents had given me for my 21st birthday and had bought a cheap, black waterproof Casio watch for £5 in Worcester.

"Does it keep good time ?", he asks.

"It's brand new !", I reply. "It's digital and seems to be split-second accurate to me."

In 1983, "digital" was a big deal. Without further ado, my Casio was pressed into service and we used this £5 novelty to navigate the oceans for the rest of our voyage.

With the sextant sighting and a precise time, the procedure for fixing our position seemed to get even more complicated and hard for me to understood. Stokie led me down to his cabin, sat at the captain's table where an ocean chart was unrolled and he selected a logarithm table from the wooden slots in front of him. With an A4 pad, biro, log chart, calculator and the sighting that I had written down, he silently and methodically started to perform line after line of mathematical calculations, slowly filling the paper as he worked downwards. His concentration was intense and not a word was spoken.

Finally, he looked up at me and smiled wordlessly. He cleared the paperwork from on top of the chart, selected a long nautical ruler from the back of the desk, a set square and a pencil and began to measure from the top of the chart. He made a small horizontal mark. Then, he worked from the left-hand side and seconds later, made another mark vertically intersecting the other one.

"There !", he pronounced.

I looked to where he was pointing and saw a pencil cross, 160 miles east of the last island in the Caribbean. I was deeply impressed at his skill and felt that I had been inducted into a hidden world. I was amazed by his ability to complete a page of complex mathematical calculations using logarithm tables and a slide rule, in a pitching yacht.

Day 3 - Friday, 11th March:

We were blessed with favourable south-easterly winds and we maintained a comfortable, if pedestrian, 5 knots per hour. My sea sickness faded and the sunburn healed quickly. Although the regular application of a bucket of sea water onto a raw wound was excruciating, its healing power was extraordinary and amazingly, left me with no scar.

Scouse became the next victim, succumbing to prickly heat, a condition where the pores of the skin become blocked and the person is unable to sweat. He became groggy and his eyelids, lips and throat glands swelled alarmingly. "If he gets much worse, we'll have to turn back" said Stokie. This proved to be the closest thing to sympathy anyone got on the trip. Allowing anyone to wallow in self-pity and miss their duties put an extra strain on other members of the crew so the atmosphere always seemed superficially callous and uncaring. Much of this stemmed from Stokie's army background and undoubtedly, it was a good thing, putting a backbone of discipline and resolve into us.

The day ended with great unease. Would we be forced to turn back so early ?

Day 4 - Saturday, 12th March:

I woke early, to a new sensation of the yacht rolling in the swell. It was by no means unpleasant in itself but I dressed quickly and strode up onto the deck to escape the sea sickness that started as soon as I planted my feet on the cabin floor and sat upright. As soon as I could see the far horizon, my equilibrium returned and the nausea faded in seconds.

Looking to the north, I saw lightning flashing several miles away under darkening clouds and realised that this deterioration in the weather was good for us. The boat was powering through the water strongly and the sails and the rigging were producing a humming noise in unison. A finely-tuned machine working at its optimal.

To our huge relief, Scouse had recovered and was back on form. The best indicator of his health and humour proved to be how frequently he called Stokie a "red-nosed bastard". As the insult count went up, Stokie and I exchanged knowing glances and knew that we wouldn't need to turn back !

A container ship appeared from the west behind us and slowly overhauled us, taking a parallel track eastwards. It was more than a mile away but I could tell that it was massive. How flimsy our yacht seemed by comparison. I watched as it sliced effortlessly through the ocean, as if the worsening weather was having absolutely no impact upon it. Stokie ducked down into his cabin and tried to raise it on the VHF maritime radio for a weather report but was answered only by static.

"That's not good", he said grimly. "We are only a mile away and we cannot even talk to a ship that's nearly alongside us".

What he meant was that if we got into any trouble, that radio wasn't going to help save us.

By 9am, the worsening weather forced us to stop sailing. The wind had risen to 40 knots and even under a small amount of sail, the yacht listed heavily to port so that its rails were awash with foam as it charged up each large wave and crashed down into the next one. The rolling sea added to the general unpleasantness.

Progressively, we took down more and more sail until we were left with a mainsail that had been reduced to barely a pocket handkerchief compared to what was unfurled two hours previously. Any attempt to sail now would result in us tearing our rather fragile and ageing sails – we could see that the jib had started to fray visibly in the last few hours. The boat was quieter and moving more slowly through the waves. We were making little progress but were clearly safer.

This storm continued, forcing us to give up all pretence of sailing and "lay a hull" which involved lashing the wheel over to point the boat into wind and leaving only a very amount of sail aloft to keep the boat stable. All that could be done was to sit below decks and wait for the high winds to lessen.

We were still at considerable risk from other ships that were much less likely to see us in the troughs of the waves and the worsening weather. So, somewhat bizarrely, we were now more likely to be run over than to drown !

We initiated a rota of keeping watch that involved sitting by the hatch for an hour at a time, dipping one's head out into the pouring rain every couple of minutes to look around the horizon for any ships. If one was sighted, you had to note its position and watch the direction and speed with which it was moving. If it got too close and there was a possible risk of collision, we would start up the engine and motor out of the path of the oncoming vessel.

We kept this up for 14 hours, running our shifts through the night, until the wind and sea had subsided and we started sailing again at dawn the next day.

Day 5 - Sunday, 13th March:

As dawn broke, it was clear that the bad weather had blown through.

We pressed on until noon and then dropped all the sails and started to motor instead. Scouse hauled the jib sail into the cockpit of the boat and began to sew up a 7-foot tear using heavy-duty needles and thread.

Inspecting the damage was a sobering experience and made us all realise that we would need to nurse Kezia all the way to Greece. The storm we had just been through was severe but should not had caused this amount of damage given our careful handling of the yacht and its sails. We were reluctant to take any more risks, only 350 miles away from Tortola.

By 3pm, although the sail was now restored and usable, the wind had dropped so much that we could only motor if we wanted to make any progress.

However, I was distracted. As we moved along at 4 knots, a delicate, fragrant floral smell started to waft across the ocean which amazed me so far from land. In a matter of minutes, we started to cross long drifts of Sargassum seaweed, each hundreds of yards in length that had floated down from the Sargasso Sea to the north of us. Its small yellow blooms shone brightly in the sunshine above a dark mass of root matter that I could make out dimly below the surface of the water. Stokie explained that it was not especially welcome – if enough of it was caught around our propeller and clogged it, one of us needed to go diving to clear it away!

In the absence of any wind that we could use to sail, we motored on until 10pm when despite an ample supply of diesel, our engine stopped without warning.

Day 7 - Tuesday 15th March 1983:

In the early hours, the yacht was just drifting silently in very light winds. Occasionally, the wind picked up enough to sail on but could drop suddenly at any moment. The sails hung limply then, flapping occasionally in the slight breeze.

This random pattern of wind was so infuriating that we no longer bothered with the effort of raising and lowering them and so we stuck to our watches, each sitting quietly alone in the night and sailing when we could, or just waiting and star gazing.

Late morning, I managed to coax the engine into life and we begin to move again to our huge relief. Two hours passed and then fuel-starved, it failed again and it was some time before I was able to trace the blockage. Impressed, Stokie bestowed upon me the title of Chief Engineer – mainly because I was the only one who could started the damnable thing and could tell the difference between the starter motor and the alternator. Also, I had found that the levers on top of the engine that controlled the flow of diesel into the cylinders had to be positioned with pinpoint accuracy before the engine would deign to start and I was the only one that could manage it.

Eventually, the wind picked up and the yacht began to speed under full sail. Our spirits lifted accordingly. We sunbathed, laughed at our change of fortune and watched dolphins playing around our bows.

Day 8 - Tuesday 16th March to Day 15 – 23rd March:

The next seven days saw the same pattern repeated: of being becalmed with no wind, engine breakdowns and repairs, hours of beautiful sailing weather and making real progress, punctuated by violent storms which forced us to stop.

The yacht log's entries reflect the frustrations, progress made and humour of each day:

00:00 "Just a joke out there."

18:00 "Tanking along, full sail."

23:00 "Zoom ! 6 knots in good style."

22:00 "From becalmed to Force 9 in 30 mins !"

00:00 "Becalmed."

04:00 "Almost a wind out there."

22:00 "Light winds doing a full circle of the compass."

00:00 "Gusting to Force 10, slowly moderated."

06:00 "German fleet vessel "Haufmann" contacted. Got our position and weather forecast."

18:00 "Stokie nearly went for an early bath when the handrail snapped."

22:00 "Going 'vell, going schnell !"

00:00 "Outran a squall – just ! A nasty-looking piece of work if I may say so."

18:00 "Wind dropped completely."

And on it went: an infuriating mix of heavy weather, perfect sailing conditions then absolutely no wind at all. With our diminishing fuel supply, we tried to avoid motoring for any more than one hour each day and then only to charge the batteries.

Increasingly as the days went past, if there was no wind, we were forced to sit and wait for it in order to save diesel.

Now, the main dispiriting factor was the lack of food. Stokie firmly believed that one meal in the evening was sufficient to keep up the strength of his crew. No breakfast, no lunch. Our average meal was a bowl of curried stew and rice, which left me feeling hungry only an hour later. There was no coffee or luxuries such as biscuits on board and I found myself with permanent indigestion. However, at least it fed the dark humour of his mutinous crew.

One mealtime, Scouse observed:

"Did you know that cockroaches can live for two months without food ?" as he crushed one scurrying about the galley floor.

"Stokie ought to take them on as crew then", I replied.

Day 16 - Thursday 24th March:

That day, we sensed a change in the weather. Two weeks out from the Caribbean and we were in the middle of the North Atlantic, some 1,200 miles from land in any direction. The enormity and bleakness of a wide expanse of ocean impressed itself upon me. We were as far away from help as we could possibly be in this hemisphere if we needed it – and the weather was definitely and steadily getting worse.

I was called from my bunk at midnight to help – all three of us were on deck as the sails needed continuous minor adjustments. We were making great speed and so the miles were ticking by but it was too much work for anyone of us to manage alone and so all of us were up, awake and working hard in the dark, being doused by sea water.

43

At 9am, the wind lessened a little and we were able to shake out the "reefs" – the folds that we tied into the sails to reduce their area and thus control our speed in severe weather.

It was a spectacular sight. We had every inch of available sail aloft and they were shining brightly in the morning sunshine. The chrome of our fittings was reflecting into our eyes. As the yacht skimmed powerfully over the waves, I felt that this was her finest moment. Coping masterfully with the ocean winds and seas, going at full pelt, sea spray funnelling up from her bows and lightly sprinkling us as we stood shoulder to shoulder around the wheel.

It was a remarkable day. Not only were we making great progress but unusually, we saw two ships, a pod of dolphins that put on a display for us and later a military transport aircraft passed low overhead – the first one we had seen in weeks.

That night, the moon was bright and full and we looked at it in wonder as we sailed.

Day 17 - Friday 25th March to Day 18 - 26th March:

Continuous gusts and squalls dogged our days. It was hard to sleep because of the continuous demands of this strenuous sailing and I felt as if I had joined the army, so unrelenting was the work. Sleep was always broken when it was at its deepest by a sudden shout:

"Rob – get up ! We need to get some sail down !".

No time to come awake. I knew that every shout of alarm had to be acted on immediately. Straight onto your feet, pull on still-wet clothes and then oilskins on top. Lastly, come the boots. Up and out onto the deck briskly. Our lives may depend on it this time. The yacht was heeling over alarmingly again and the port rail was in the water but a gentle release of one of the ropes that had been locked-off, the jib sail slackened slightly and the boat started to come upright. All these movements were done smoothly and by inches – not by dramatic, panicked and jerking actions. Releasing sheets quickly could result in entanglements and make things much worse. By now, we were all attuned to Kezia – we knew what she liked and how she responded, so we tended to her with a combined urgency and gentleness.

The next two days were punctuated by spells of brilliant sunshine, strong gusts and heavy squalls. We sailed hard and many miles slid under our keel, 160 in total, which was good for a small yacht.

Early on the 26th, we saw another ship which identified itself as a British banana boat, giving rise to many rousing choruses of "Daylight come and we want to go home". Hilarity subsided when the radio operator warned us of a low-pressure system heading our way.

"That is impossible", Stokie told him. "The barometer reads 1030, much too high".

He was still shaking his headed at the impossibility of this when a low-pressure system of 1030 arrived at 8pm and fell upon us with all its force.

Chapter Four

Playing Cards in a Hurricane

Day 19 - Sunday 27th March 1983:

In thirty minutes, the wind rose to 45 knots, Force 9 and we quickly took down sail. This brought the boat upright, made her more stable and we pressed on.

It happened to be my watch so I was at the wheel and concentrating hard. This was no time for mistakes.

With torrential rain lashing across the decks and no more to be done on the rigging, Stokie and Scouse retreated to the cover of the saloon below decks but stood by the open door and watched.

I was becoming increasingly irritated and bewildered because although I was steering carefully to the right course and the sails were filling perfectly, Kezia was intent on sliding into the troughs of waves in a different direction and rolling from side to side in a way that I had never seen before. Each time this happened, I pulled her back on course and sailed on for a few seconds before I lost control of her again. I was not afraid, just thoroughly confused. Everything I was doing had always worked before, so why not now ?

Then, I looked into the faces of Stokie and Scouse, framed in the doorway and looking intently at me. Suddenly, I felt foolish and braced myself for another round of mockery but it never came. Stokie looked at me gently and said quietly, "Give it up, Rob. Lash the wheel to port and come inside. There's nothing you can do now".

"Sailing's over for a while, gents", he said to us "but we can make ourselves safer. Grab every length of rope you can find and follow me". Under his instruction, we tied ropes to different corners and anchor points of the yacht and threw them out in different directions. They lay on the surface of the water like a giant spider's web, extending many yards outwards. "That will give us extra stability. The wet rope helps to anchor us to the spot and can help stop us capsizing. But it won't save us from the biggest waves".

Taking some comfort that we had done everything we could for now, we headed back to the warmth of the cabin but before I ducked down below, I took stock of what was happening around us. Not only was the rain lashing across the decks viciously but the wind was blasting through the rigging and sails, with a banshee howl that sounded like a wounded animal. Even more fearsome were the waves. There was no pattern or structure to them now. They had lost their form and were tumbling over and over each other from different directions and in the midst of this maelstrom, our tiny yacht bobbed and floated. Sometimes, we were deep down in the trough of a wave, looking up at sheer walls that were more than 12' above us or even more frighteningly, on top of a pinnacle of water. At the zenith, I felt that we were about to plunge downwards in an unstoppable final dive to the bottom of the ocean. Each time, we were lowered gently from this height but then pounded from every direction by waves that washed over our sides and drained away.

Resigned that I could do nothing and quietly terrified, I trudged down the steps of the saloon and slid the door closed behind me.

"What now ?" I asked.

"We wait." said Stokie. "But we must keep up with our storm watches right round the clock and keep up with the rotas –

believe it or not, we are now in even more danger of being run over by another ship".

Oh joy, I thought to myself. If the storm doesn't get us, a container ship will ! We sat around the oval, teak table in our wet gear and didn't speak. I was in awe of what I had just witnessed. I had seen the full force of the ocean and it was beyond all description. Why had I dared to think that we could sail a 35' yacht across thousands of miles of ocean and come out alive ? I thought of all the millions of men before me who had taken to the sea in cheerful willingness. Better men than me – braver, tougher, much more highly skilled – who had died in the same way.

I felt no panic. I wasn't paralysed by fear but I was resigned to the idea that I might die this day. It had been a great idea and a wonderful adventure but we really had taken a risk too far. But there was nothing any of us could do it about it, we were in this situation now and all we could do was to try and stay alive.

So we embarked upon a new routine. Whoever was on watch got up from their seat every five minutes, opened the top hatch and scanned carefully around the complete 360° horizon, pausing to look beyond massive waves to make sure that they were not hiding a ship that was heading towards us. We did this for two hours and then it was the next person's turn.

All the while, the wind speed continued to increase. It was noticeable in the yacht because its shrill shrieking seemed to keep on rising in pitch slowly. Stokie rose from his seat, put on his waterproof jacket and went outside for several minutes. When he came back, he looked grim-faced.

"What's happening ?", I asked.

"Well, it's up to Force 11 now. I've been checking the wind speed, the height of the waves and looking at how the crests are behaving. We are talking near hurricane force now. Wind is about 70 miles an hour and the waves are at least 40 feet."

"Right, let's get ready", he said at last.

A decision had been made. He pulled the life-raft out into the middle of the saloon floor from its stowage under the stairs. It was still packed and sealed up in its white fibreglass box like an outsized suitcase. He unravelled a long, yellow strap from its side and made sure that it was free of any tangles. It put me in mind of a ripcord on a parachute and I realised that it would indeed serve a similar purpose when the time came.

He reached back and handed me a sealed, blue plastic container that looked like an oversized sweet jar, with a handle.

"Rob, you are in charge of the flares. Guard them with your life from now on."

"Scouse, collect all the food that you can carry. Put it in a polythene bag, leave a bit of air in it so that it will float, seal it up and make it watertight. Keep it right by you. From now on, you're in charge of food."

He sat down on top of the life-raft with his back to the toilet and with his orders given, was content to wait.

I had to ask the question.

"So, when do we go then ?"

"We don't." said Stokie. "Not as long as this boat is floating, even if it's half under water, it will still be better than any life-raft. If the time comes, I will smash the life-raft through the doors and go with it, out over the side. You stay right on my heels and do exactly what I do."

I really wish I hadn't asked now.

We sat in the dark, facing in towards each other, waiting for the crash of a monstrous wave that would be the death knell of our yacht. This would be our call to action and each of us knew what we would do when we abandoned ship. We would do this with speed and precision. Stokie had the life-raft, I had the flares, Scouse had the food. We sat like this for many hours, awake and looking at each other wordlessly, right through the night.

PLAYING CARDS IN A HURRICANE

When daylight came, the wind, sea and waves were still as violent and monstrous but we felt that we had been spared. None of us mentioned it but the mood became lighter. We went out onto the deck, adjusted the rigging, took stock and could find no damage.

Thoroughly soaked again, we retreated back down below again and settled into a new routine together. Cooking, brewing tea and coffee, playing many hands of cards, listening to music but always keeping watch. Never in my life before had I played cards this much, nor ever since. Whist, Rummy, Scabby Queen, Blackjack, Egyptian Ratscrews, Crazy Eights. There seemed to be no end to the games, nor Scouse's encyclopedic knowledge of them. If one of us didn't know the next one that he announced, he would teach it to us patiently and clearly. He avoided only Cribbage and Poker because we needed a board with pegs, or money, and we had neither !

This went on for two days, punctuated only by two waves at different times that hit the yacht with such force that it reverberated like a drum, shuddering for several seconds after each wave had long gone.

In the end, it was not the storm but the monotony of living like this that nearly killed us. Unnoticed by us, Scouse had become increasingly lax in keeping watch and when at last he did look out and then around, he yelped in surprise. Stokie and I raced to the hatch and there amongst the rolling 40' waves was a container vessel, a few hundred yards away. It was massive and charged through the waves as if they were of no consequence. It was converging on our course but thankfully, it was clear that it wouldn't come close after all. The air turned blue as we expressed our displeasure to Scouse and for once, there was not an ounce of humour behind it.

Stokie raced to the radio and tried to hail the ship for a weather forecast and a position. The ship was so close and yet there was no answer to his repeated and urgent calling. Then, I looked up and all became clear.

Only one part of the yacht had been damaged – the storm had completely ripped away our VHF radio aerial. It was gone and now we couldn't talk to anyone or call for help.

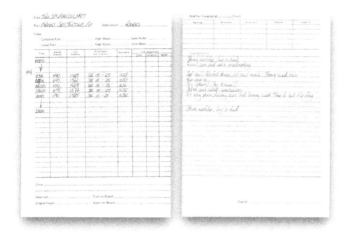

Another two days passed without incident and the storm subsided ever so slowly. We were out of danger. At 6.30am on April Fool's Day, we were able to set sail again and how very apt this seemed to us. Fools who appeared to have got away with it.

With the first glimpse of the sun, Stokie reached for his sextant and managed to find our position. It turned out that in the five days of the storm, we had drifted 35 miles to the south-east. Thankfully, it was in the right general direction.

Day 25 - Saturday 2nd April 1983:

That glimpse of the sun proved to be short-lived, we sailed on under heavy cloud and occasional squalls that left us soaked through again.

A grim resolve had settled in and we were forging ahead, hardly speaking because we were so focused on reaching the islands of the Azores quickly. We had been so intent on getting through the last week that we had hardly noticed our other problems – and they were severe.

The switch-gear that controlled both the engine speed and the reverse and forward gears had been getting harder to use in recent days. It was difficult to get its handle to go into gear. If it should fail and then the wind dropped, we would be powerless. This would put us in a dangerous situation if we couldn't manoeuvre when we neared land in the next day, or if a ship got too close and we needed to escape in a different direction.

Our drinking water was contaminated with a chemical taste and smell. It was perfectly acceptable in tea or coffee but foul to drink from the tap. We discussed it and surmised that the worst case was if there was a dead animal or some insects decomposing in the main tank which was beneath the bench seats in the saloon. Whilst at sea, we were in no position to undo all of the many screws that sealed it. We would have to wait until we reached port before we could investigate properly and decided that we should only drink it boiled from the kettle for our safety.

PLAYING CARDS IN A HURRICANE

Worst of all, we were now really hungry and nearly out of supplies. We had tea, coffee and powdered milk to flavour our contaminated water but all we had left to eat was a string bag containing onions and an unopened jar of mayonnaise. Even Scouse's wonderfully inventive culinary skills couldn't combine these into a full and satisfying meal for three working men. Stokie's precise calculations of the rations that we would need to cross the North Atlantic back in Tortola had made no allowance for sitting in a storm without moving for several days.

When we had planned our Atlantic crossing back in David Blackwell's cottage, we had planned to make our first stop in the port of Horta on the island of Faial, one of the larger and more developed islands of the Azores, an archipelago of nine islands lying 850 miles off the west coast of Portugal. Ideally, that was still our main objective for getting fresh food and doing any repairs necessary.

It was clear to us that getting to Horta in our current state would be a major challenge now. Stokie called us down to his cramped aft cabin, where we pored over his large ocean chart and saw the Azores stretching out over 370 miles south-eastwards, in a long chain. We were within striking distance of Flores, the most westward of the islands but getting into its tiny fishing harbour would be extremely risky in rough seas and we knew that we needed complicated repairs. Would we find a workshop or an engineer there? The alternative was to tighten our belts and sail on to Horta for another two days at sea, knowing that this would be the better solution to all our problems.

We discussed this at length and in the end, the deciding factor was our faulty switch-gear. If we found ourselves stuck half-way to Horta with no engine, no wind with which to sail by and no food, our situation would become very serious.

"It's Flores then, guys." proclaimed Stokie at last.

"It could be quite hairy getting in but hopefully, we can call the locals up for some help if we get stuck."

Yes, some hope without a VHF aerial, I thought to myself.

We sailed on for many long, hungry hours until at midday, I saw a seam of black cloud far off on the horizon but at a strangely low altitude. It remained stationary and looked so out of place that I called Stokie up to have a look.

He stepped up, looked to where I was pointing and immediately shouted "Land Ho !" in an excited, salty sea-dog fashion.

"You can see land ?"

"Nope, not yet but that's exactly what that is. You often see that phenomenon at sea – cloud sticking to the land like that. It must be Corvo – it's in exactly the right place."

At this, I felt the hairs on the back of my neck stand up. Before I came on this trip, I had finished reading a book called "The Airmen Who Would Not Die" by John Fuller. In it, he tells the story of an early English aviator, Captain Raymond Hinchliffe, who attempts to be the first to fly to America in a small propeller plane but drowns in the attempt. His anguished soul then begins to make contact with a lady medium during a séance in London. "Can you help a drowning man ?" he begins. He is confused and cannot understood where he is. His overriding worry is for his widow and little daughter who do not know of his fate. Over several weeks, after the widow rebuffs the medium many times in fear and disbelief, the husband and wife are reunited in the séance room where he tells her precisely where to find the life insurance documents that she has been searching for in desperation. Whilst no happy ending, in the end comes understanding, acceptance and some measure of comfort for them all. And where does he tell them that he crashed into the sea and died ? Corvo, in the islands of the Azores and so this happened to be our very first sight of land in many weeks. The "Island of the Crow". A dark, foreboding place watched over by a solitary cloud. We sailed on towards Flores, now only hours away.

Finally, in pitch darkness, we found ourselves two miles off the north-eastern coast of Flores, drifting, becalmed. Stokie turned the ignition key in the cockpit, started the engine and then reached down to move the switch-gear lever forward.

"It's jammed." he said, turning expectantly to me in my capacity as Chief Engineer.

With five years' experience of working in engineering factories and working on cars, I was confident that I could free it but in an instant, as I gripped the lever, I realised that not only was it unmoving, it had now seized solid. There was no way that the lever would ever move again without repair and exactly as we had feared last night, we were now drifting without wind and power, perilously close to land. Thankfully, without any wind or a strong current, the yacht sat exactly where it was and wasn't obviously drifting into danger. Once again, we could do nothing but wait.

Again, it was my turn to be on watch so Stokie and Scouse retired down into the saloon and left me alone on deck. It was incredibly frustrating to be so close to a warm meal and rest. I could see the lights of fishermens' cottages on the shoreline distinctly, warm, welcoming and out of reach. I felt my anger and irritation rising with the sheer impotence of our situation. I decided to ask Stokie if there was anything we could do to try and raise help.

I took hold of the right wooden door, swung it open as I had done many times before and it came clean off its hinges. Stokie and Scouse looked up blankly from the cabin below, to see me holding it in my hand. It occurred to me that this door was supposed be watertight and keep us safe if the boat should capsize.

"This fucking boat will be the death of us all." I exploded.

I was at the end of my tether with exhaustion, starvation and cold but I had sufficient control to realise that if I launched this now useless piece of wood over the side as I desperately wanted to, it would be very hard to replace later. So I threw it down onto the cockpit floor and watched it skid safely to the back and stop with a bang.

"Yeah, it's a crock, mate." said Scouse seeing my desperation. "Let me take over for a while".

As he headed out into the cockpit to keep watch, I launched myself onto my bunk fully clothed and lay there for a few seconds before falling into a deep and grateful sleep.

Day 26 - Sunday 3rd April 1983:

I awoke at first light and we had drifted further down the coast on the eastern side of Flores. A gentle wind filled the sails which were flapping limply but were giving us a little propulsion forwards. As I emerged on deck and looked around, I couldn't help but smile broadly. It looked almost as if we had lost our way and arrived off the coast of Wales. Difficult though our situation was, I marvelled at the beauty and bright, verdant greenery of the mountainous island, now no more than a mile away. I had expected islands in the middle of the Atlantic to be barren, treeless and grey, blasted as they were by storms and sea water. How wrong I was!

Eventually, we drifted parallel to the tiny fishing harbour of Santa Cruz and it was clear to all of us that we had a very serious problem. The entrance was guarded by two large pillars of rock, left and right and the waves were coursing through the small gap in a spray of white foam, before they broke upon the concrete slipway used to launch the fishing boats. The safe area of the harbour lay behind a sea wall and to get into that area, we would need to power through the foaming water of the entrance and then make a sharp right turn into the quiet water behind the wall. All must be attempted under sail as our engine was still useless without the switch-gear.

I was confident in Stokie's ability to steer us through the tiny gap but if a rogue wave hit us at the wrong moment, we would be dashed against the rocks and destroyed.

We hadn't seen a soul in the small town so far. There was no sign of life and it looked as if the fishermen had decided that they would not venture out to sea in these winds and high waves. The boatyard doors were firmly closed and no boats could be seen. Some distance behind us, we saw another white yacht following us down the channel and given the remoteness of the location, it was clear that they were also seeking safe haven in Santa Cruz too.

Helpless, we dropped all our sails and sat safely away from the harbour entrance. Stokie decided to try the radio again. We may not have a VHF aerial but we were so close to the boatyard, it was worth a try. Failing that we had distress flares.

"Santa Cruz, Santa Cruz, this is the sailing yacht Kezia of Tortola in need of assistance. Please respond."

Instantly, the radio crackled in response and a heavily-accented voice replies.

"Yes, we hear you Kezia, what is your situation ?"

To a man, the three of us jumped for joy, punching the air with exhilaration at this small success.

"Santa Cruz, we have lost our engine and are only under sail so we cannot risk the entrance. We are out of food and urgently needed repairs – we cannot make it to Faial. Is it possible for someone to tow us into your harbour please ?"

"Yes, Kezia, I will come. Wait where you are, it will take time."

We sat down in the cockpit, smiling broadly at each other. We knew that getting into the harbour, even under tow, was going to be dangerous but our desperation had made us determined. No going back now.

So we waited for an interminable time. We saw a group of six distant figures assemble in the street beyond the harbour and watched as they headed towards the boatyard doors. These must be our would-be saviours. Methodically and carefully, we saw them haul a large wooden launch out into the daylight on its trailer. They spent several minutes checking it and making preparations that we couldn't see clearly. At last, three men climbed into the boat on land and the other three operated a winch that reeled out a larger hawser attached to the front of the launch. All the while, waves were crashing up the slipway and we could see that all the men were getting soaked and putting themselves in danger, even at this distance.

With painful slowness, the boat inched down the concrete runway until it floated clear of its steel trailer which disappeared beneath the boiling sea. One crewman strode confidently to the bow of the boat and let the rope go with a swift, deft movement. The boat reversed backwards powerfully and turned quickly with its bow pointing out to the harbour entrance.

We stiffened as we watched the little wooden boat pause for a few seconds, as if readying itself for launch. And suddenly, it did. Its skipper pushed the throttle handle forwards, it sprung powerfully to life and surged towards the foaming harbour entrance. Within seconds, it was safely through the gap and began a slow arc northward to where we were lying offshore.

Some minutes later, the green wooden boat drew alongside and we got our first glimpse of men of the Azores. Tall, strong, swarthy, rough-hewn men who looked as if they had spent their whole lives at sea – which they had. Their commander was a man of around sixty-five, with a shock of swept-back white hair and he barked instructions in Portuguese to his two crewmates.

A heavy kemp rope was thrown across the gap between the two boats. Stokie caught this and walked this along the deck to the point of the bow and bent down. He tied this firmly to the steel anchor housing on the prow of the yacht and straightened up.

The Portuguese captain brought the launch up slightly so that he and Stokie were only ten feet apart.

"Our harbour is very difficult", he shouted across, "We have one chance only."

"When we go in, we must turn immediately to the right together, very sharp. If you don't, we will crash. You understand ?"

Stokie nodded. It would be very risky and might end in ruin, no matter how skillfully the turn was executed. The captain looked into Stokie's eyes as if to size him up for the task ahead and there was a silent communion between them. There was a flicker in the man's eyes as if to say "Yes, you'll do", he turned the wheel and his boat inched back towards the harbour slowly.

Everyone watched the rope intently as it tightened between the two boats. When it was completely taught, we felt the latent power of the launch as it jerked us forward and then powered smoothly towards the harbour entrance. We were now moving at speed – a greater speed than we would normally achieve either under sail or our own power but we knew it would be necessary if we were to pass through the eye of the needle and find that patch of safe water beyond the wall.

We exchanged glances and as we had found during the worst moments during the storm, no-one said a word. We were focused, watchful and concentrating, waiting for any sudden breakage or some new danger and we continued to speed towards the town of Santa Cruz directly ahead of us.

And the moment came when we were at the point of no return, we were surging into the harbour entrance and we held our breath, as one.

The moment that the captain's boat passed the rock on the right side, he wrenched it into a hard turn to the right and Stokie executed the same manoeuvre, five seconds later, in perfect synchronisation. Suddenly, the drama was over. We were in ! We'd done it !

The green launch slowed and turned down our port side and we slowed just as abruptly – we were in quiet water and almost stationary. I looked up and there were about ten men standing all around us, high up on the harbour walls, with ropes in their hands in readiness. Again, I felt that I had walked into a highly-drilled, military scenario. I ran to the bow of the boat, untied the heavy tow rope and threw it back to one of their crewmen. Simultaneously, a cascade of lines dropped onto our deck, thrown by the fishermen around us which we tied urgently to the cleats and stanchions on every corner of the yacht. Within seconds, with the ropes now tightened by the men on the walls around us, we were like a fly trapped in a spider's web extending in all directions. We were unable to move by even a fraction but unlike the fly, we were now safe.

Instantly, the focus of the town's men now turned to the other yacht, waiting its turn, a hundred yards away from the harbour entrance. The green launch turned towards the open sea and powered out through the surf again on its next mission. Scouse, Stokie and I busied ourselves on Kezia's deck, tidying away the sails and ropes. Again, this was unspoken. We kept to our sailing discipline and even although we had just been rescued, we wanted the local seamen to see that we were professional and proud of it.

Within minutes, the other yacht, a French Beneteau, had also been safely towed into port in exactly the same way. The fishermen drew her up behind us and again, she was pinioned by many ropes stretching out in different directions to the harbour walls – she had her very own spider's web like us. She was longer, more modern and sleek than us but she was just as helpless as we were.

Busy on deck, I heard the sound of a powerful outboard motor and looked up towards the boatyard doors. A large black

Zodiac inflatable had been launched from the slipway and was speeding towards us. It drew alongside and once again, it was our white-haired Captain but he was beaming widely now and looking very relaxed.

"Come, English !" he said. "Our work is done for today. Get in the boat !"

Once again, we were immensely grateful and obliged to him. We had no inflatable of our own and were completely dependent on the kindness and help of these fishermen. We climbed down carefully into the inflatable which had ample room for all four of us and within ten seconds, we were drawing up to the inner harbour wall. Each of us leaped nimbly across the gap and climbed the sea-washed stone steps to the top as the Zodiac turned back to collect the Frenchmen.

As I took my first proper steps on land for one month, my legs nearly gave way. I was shocked and amused by how weak my legs had become – they could barely support my weight. I looked to the others and they too were walking like geriatric cowboys. So we wobbled unsurely across the stone flags of the harbour towards the boatyard together, laughing at each other's infirmity.

The boatyard door was the informal meeting point for everyone that had just been involved in the drama: the fishermen who had been casting ropes and securing them across the harbour and the French yachtsmen who arrived with us. We shook hands warmly with everyone present and finally, we were introduced to our saviours. The white-haired captain was Ernesto and his two sons that were on-board the green boat were Raoul and Lourenco. With a new-found, courtly grace, Stokie spoke for all of us:

"Ernesto, we are truly grateful for your help and for your sons' help, in getting us safely into your harbour this morning. We would have been in great trouble without you. We thank you sincerely."

The wily, old silver-tongued charmer, I thought. I couldn't had put it better myself.

"My friend, this is what sailors do for each other. You would had done the same for us !"

I was impressed that almost all of the local people seemed able to speak English to differing degrees. I would never have expected that in a small, far-flung island community.

For a time, we stood and talked with them, sharing cigarettes, explaining who we were, what we were attempting to do and what had happened until now. We ignored the drizzle and cold wind, they were nothing to us now. The fishermen listened to our story, nodded and smiled and seemed unsurprised. Men had lived on the Azores for thousands of years and they were at one with the sea. These men were hardened sailors and had seen everything that we had – and undoubtedly much more.

After a while, with more handshakes and our repeated thanks, Stokie, Scouse and I left them and started to walk up the steep, cobbled main street, crowded with old traditional cottages lining each side.

"Come on boys." said Stokie. "I'll treat you to a slap-up meal. I think we all deserve it."

Things were indeed looking up, I thought to myself.

Chapter Five

Mutiny in the Azores

That day in 1983, there was something beautifully rustic and unspoiled about Santa Cruz, compared to the modern rush of Florida that we had left behind us only a few short weeks previously. I felt that I had wandered onto the film set of a scene set in a fishing village in the 19th century. I couldn't see a car, a TV aerial or even a doorbell on the cottages that we were walking past. Even in my dazed state, I took in the white-washed plaster walls of the cottages as we passed by, their beautifully brightly-painted wooden doors, the cobbled road beneath our feet. This wonderful place was truly unspoiled.

Or perhaps I was just overwhelmingly grateful to be on dry land again after all we had been through. We were still incredibly hungry. Not a morsel had passed our lips in many hours but we had been caught up in the moment – a moment that had lasted several hours. There had been danger this day and bursts of frenetic activity. We had talked to the local people at length and not for one moment had I thought of food.

We reached the top of the street, turned left and within yards we saw a restaurant in an old stone building on the left. We turned down its stone-flag path, I pulled open the front door with its bottle-glass panes and gestured for my colleagues to enter with a courtly bow.

Although it was only mid-morning, we were made welcome by the landlord and solitary waitress for an early lunch. I thought they could sense our quiet desperation because they didn't question our need for a hearty meal at this early hour or perhaps word about us had got around this small town already. We ordered steak, chips and beer which were a revelation after many weeks of canned minced meat, peas and rice. Surprisingly, although we were literally starving, we didn't eat ravenously or over-order. With much shrunken stomachs, a single, large plate of food was more than satisfactory and absolutely delicious.

Considering all the stresses and strains that we had been through and how we had lived cheek by jowl for so many weeks, we enjoyed a surprisingly relaxed and jovial lunch and were easy in each other's company. The sense of relief and celebration was almost tangible.

As soon as the meal was over, we made our excuses. There were phone calls home to be made and we wandered off in different directions, each of us eager to have his own space. We agreed to meet back at the boatyard at 2 pm.

Back out on the street again, I meandered through the narrowed streets and chance upon a gleaming white church, tall, thin and angular. Without a moment's hesitation or even a conscious thought of what I was doing, I stepped over the threshold and walked into the empty building. I hadn't been in a church for seven years but I walked purposefully to the front and slid into an old oak pew, right at the front in the centre, facing the altar. I sank to my knees, clasped my hands together and prayed fervently, giving thanks that I had been saved. How else could we had lived through all that without God's help ? It was unthinkable, not possible. I stayed on my knees for a considerable time giving thanks. Finally, somewhat reluctantly, I stood up and walked out.

I kept my solitary visit to the church that day a secret from Stokie and Scouse, either because I was embarrassed or thought they would not understand. Then, one afternoon later, sailing in the sunshine under blue skies many weeks later, we admitted to each other that we all had sat alone in that church that same afternoon and said our prayers of thanks.

Meanwhile, I continued my stroll around the back streets of Santa Cruz and chanced upon a telephone box. Luckily, I had received many coins in change back at the restaurant and now sorted it into nicely-ordered piles along the top of its wall-mounted box, knowing that I needed a small fortune for what I was about to do. I lifted the receiver, pushed in the first of the coins and dialed my home number.

I heard the phone ringing in a European dial tone and then my Mum's voice said,

"Good morning, Red Lion."

"Mum, it's me, it's Rob ! I've reached the Azores, we're safe !"

I wanted to make those first words clear and unambiguous so that if we got cut off, she would know the important part.

"Oh Rob, that's wonderful ! We've been so worried about you, no news for so long but here you are! That's such a relief ! What's happened ? Where are you exactly ?"

In those days without mobile phones, fax machines, email or social media, a coin-operated payphone was the most sophisticated way of calling home. It was only in the years to come that I truly appreciated the fear and worry that my parents must had felt in those weeks when I was completely out of contact, in mid-Atlantic.

We chatted for several minutes and I reassured her that the worst was now over. I would be late home by several weeks but I was sure we would make it, although I told her this more in hope than certainty. We had a damaged yacht that needed urgent repair before we could sail on but I didn't tell her that. Neither did I tell her that I spent one night sitting by a life-raft recently, waiting to abandon ship. I promised that I would call her when I reached our next port very soon, telling her not to worry now and then, I rang off.

Next, I rang my friend Terry who was getting married next month whose wedding invitation I had cheerfully accepted a while back:

"Mate, you know when I said something would have to have gone seriously wrong if I'm not back in three months ?"

"Yep, you must be well on your way to Corfu by now."

"Er no. Not exactly. I'm really sorry but I'm not going to be back in time for your wedding."

I explained everything that had happened and this time I didn't leave out the scary bits.

"Can't be helped, Rob", said Terry. "Look on the bright side, you could write a book about all this one day !"

Much relieved that I had managed to get through to everyone that I needed to, I trudged back down to the harbour in time for the planned rendezvous.

As I reached where Stokie and Scouse were standing together, Stokie burst out enthusiastically:

"Rob, good news ! I've found an engineer to fix the morse gear ! And even better than that, Raoul had offered us a spare bedroom, up there, looking out over the yacht so we can keep an eye on her!"

I looked up to where he was pointing and there was indeed a third-floor attic room facing out over the harbour, in the building that we were standing next to. This felt like a great result. It was clear that the morse gear would take a few days to fix, meanwhile we would get to sleep in beds on dry land !

We borrowed the Zodiac inflatable, headed back to Kezia and moored up alongside her. Whilst Stokie and Scouse checked over all the mooring lines again, re-securing and tightening them, I disconnected the broken morse gear from its housing in the cockpit. Each of us packed a small bag containing fresh clothes, a towel, toiletries, a sleeping bag and personal items. We locked the cabin up again and headed back across the harbour. I had the morse gear safely stowed under my jacket. Once this had been delivered to the engineer's workshop, we headed back to our new quarters in the room that Raoul had lent to us.

As the three of us climbed up to the attic and stepped into the room, my heart sank. Not only was it spartan and neglected but there was only one ancient double bed with an iron stead. It was more of a storeroom than a bedroom but at least, it was a clean, dry room onshore. We were extremely grateful for the kindness.

Later in the afternoon, we ate a light snack at a local café and as night fell, we headed back to the room to retire.

"Right, lads. Who is going to take the first watch ?" said Stokie.

Caught completely by surprise, Scouse and I looked at each other blankly and then both turned to Stokie to see if he was joking.

"Sorry, not with you, boss" said Scouse. "We are on dry land. Why would we want to do that? Not too many ships around here that I can see."

Stokie paced to the window, looking out of the window across the harbour to where Kezia was sitting in the twilight. He looked nervously around him and almost muttered:

"You don't understand, you don't understand. This stuff is important. If she goes down, we need to know at exactly what time for the insurance company. She's my responsibility"

"So... talking hypothetically like," said Scouse quizzically, raising an eyebrow in my direction. "If she goes down while we're asleep, why don't we just... make up a time ?" he said with dramatic effect.

"No. No. No." said Stokie, speaking quickly and nervously. "That won't do at all. We shall have to keep up the watches right through the night. I'm responsible. I'm the skipper. If you expect to sail on with me, you'll both do as you're told."

Scouse and I both sighed loudly in exasperation. What new madness was this ? We were both so exhausted that I thought quietly to myself that it would be a blessing if the damned thing did sink. Someone would have to fly us home then.

So, I found myself standing at the window at 2am, looking out over the harbour in the moonlight watching over Kezia as she bucked on rough waves but still refused to sink, whilst the other two snored loudly - Scouse from the iron bed and Stokie, in his sleeping bag in a corner on the floor.

Two hours later, we switched on our night watch and I retired to my sleeping bag, still shaking my head at the madness of keeping watch over a boat whilst onshore.

The cold light of day normally brings reason but not on this day. We headed back up the hill to the little café and ordered coffee and pastries. Once we were settled, Stokie dropped his bombshell.

"OK. I've been thinking about this all night", he said. I was impressed that he could both snore and strategise at the same time. "The trip ends here. That boat isn't seaworthy and never has been. We should never have left Tortola. I'm not going to risk our lives anymore. I'm not prepared to carry on. It's over. I'm going to ring David and break the news. Don't worry, you'll be looked after. He will get you home."

Scouse and I were deeply shocked. Not because Stokie was wrong in anything he was saying but it was a major decision to suddenly abandon ship. What would happen to the yacht ? How would we get back to the European mainland with no money, let alone make it back to England ?

We discussed the situation for the next hour, with Scouse and I urging him to get the boat fixed and carry on but Stokie was calm and his mind was made up.

"I'll give David time to wake up and then I'll call and tell him." he said.

Good luck with that, I thought to myself.

Stokie stepped up from the table and left us to pay the bill. He strode towards the door and left like a man on a mission, which of course, he was.

"So... the mad bugger had organised his own One Man Mutiny then !" said Scouse.

We shook our heads, grinning in disbelief at what had just unfolded.

Within the hour, Stokie was back in the café, standing at our table.

"OK. So I told David straight. No way was I sailing that pile of crap another mile. We talked it through and he said just to hold on, he's going to get on a plane right away, come here and help us sort things out but I said, that's fine but I won't be skippering it anymore."

"How the heck is he going to get here ?" I asked. "The airport is a grass landing strip, only good for a propeller plane. He is going to have to fly out to Portugal and then charter a smaller plane, if he comes."

"Not my problem, mate."

We settled into a pattern of some form of normality for the next four days, spending much of our time, drinking coffee and smoking in the café. We continued to stay in the small attic room as before. Stokie quietly dropped the bizarre watch-keeping rota and Scouse and I didn't mention it either for fear that he would try to revive it.

Exploring around the town, we found the townspeople very welcoming. They would often stop to welcome us and ask about our travels. In this way, we met a delightful couple, Alfredo and Maria, who were the local schoolteachers and they invited us to dinner at their home one night. We had a wonderful evening, Maria cooked superbly for us and there was much wine and great conversation. It was lovely for us to be we welcomed into their home, talk about their lives and the Azores. Equally, they were interested to hear about our lives in England and of course, our recent adventure. Late in the evening, I disgraced myself by falling soundly asleep whilst sitting upright at the table and fell backwards off the wooden bench on which I was seated. I woke to the startled realisation that I was holding myself up on one hand that I could only have flung out instinctively before I hit the stone floor. That said, I realised that this could only be down to complete exhaustion. I made my sincere apologies, explained myself and moved to leave. Alfredo and Maria were warm and understanding, I said my goodbyes and headed off into the night to sleep on the old iron bed.

PLAYING CARDS IN A HURRICANE

On the Sunday, we were collected by Raoul and taken off to watch a local football match which most of the town seemed to have turned out for. It was a hard-fought match, played to a good standard but most of all, I was impressed that they managed to play on such lumpy, rough ground that was more akin to a patch of Dartmoor than any football pitch I had ever seen.

With the promise of fine weather the next day and on Alfredo's recommendation, I decided to hike out to the Reserva Florestal Natural in the centre of the island, a beautiful national park focused around the Morro Alto mountain. At 3,000 ft, this was the highest peak on the island and a long extinct volcano. Stokie and Scouse decided that it wasn't for them and stayed behind. Getting there was hard walking: a steady eight-mile ascent up to 2,000 ft that took me three hours each way. However, when I reached the Reserve, the view richly repaid all my efforts. The verdant green landscape was beautiful in its own right but its large volcanic craters each contained lakes with black, green or completely clear water. These were the Lagoa Negra, Comprida, Seca and Branca. I decided it was the most wild and beautiful place that I had even seen in the world. The walk back to Santa Cruz was a pleasure. Not only was it downhill all the way but I was much buoyed by what I had seen and achieved.

Every day without fail, Stokie walked down to the engineer's workshop to ask how he was getting on with the repair of the morse gear, although he continued to restate his determination never to sail on Kezia ever again. The answer was always the same '....just a few more days'.

At last, David arrived from London, having taken a flight down from Heathrow to Lisbon and then catching a light aircraft to Santa Cruz.

We greeted him warmly in the restaurant and after a few minutes, he turned to Stokie and said:

"Right, let's go through everything and we'll sort this out. Guys, leave us to it for a while, the beers are on me."

With that, David and Stokie headed into a small private dining room and shut the door, leaving Scouse and I at the table.

"Feels like a flippin' Arab - Israeli Summit!" I said to Scouse.

An hour later, David emerged by himself, headed over to our table and sat down to tell us of the outcome of their discussion. Stokie remained behind in the private room.

"Guys, I am sorry you've had such a hard time of it recently. Stokie and I have agreed that the trip will continue just as we planned originally. Can we count on you both of you to see it through ?"

Scouse and I didn't hesitate. As long as we could get the boat properly fixed up, we had done the hard bit and I quite fancied seeing the Mediterranean in late Spring. We explained this to him and he replied:

"Well, thanks, lads. I am really grateful to you and I know that Stokie is too. As a gesture of appreciation and so that you have got some spending money while we wait for the repairs, please have this." He formally handed £50 to each of us which seemed like a small fortune then. We gratefully accepted the cash and assured him that we would stick it out to the end.

Looking relieved and satisfied that all had been resolved, David left us sitting at the table and headed back to his hotel. Minutes later, Stokie emerged from the back room and joined us at the table. He was hard to read, neither looking fearful, angry or for that matter, particularly happy.

"So..." I ventured. "David tells us that you've agreed to carry on after all. How did he convince you, then?"

Stokie sighed.

"Well, he said to me, 'How could you give up when you've come so far? You've done the hardest bit. The Med will be a walk in the park. It's nothing compared to what you've just managed.' And of course, he is right. And if I walk away now, it would be the first time that I have ever failed to complete anything that I set out to do in my life and I could't have that. I still think the boat is a crock of shit but we will get it repaired and we will carry on to Corfu."

He rose to leave.

"And then he threatened to break my legs if I didn't finish the job."

David left the next day and flew back to London, apparently confident that we would indeed be sailing on. I was not convinced. Not because I thought Stokie was going to renege on the agreement but because our boatyard engineer was still saying "just a few more days". I wondered what the Portuguese translation of "mañana" was ? Would we ever leave ?

The weather was foul and we could not have set sail that day even if the yacht suddenly and magically became sea-worthy. After several hours spent sitting and drinking coffee in the steamed-up café, Stokie suggested that we headed back over to the yacht and repair the broken hatch door which would have to be done sometime. Increasingly bored of hanging around town on another wet afternoon, we readily agreed, despite the rough seas.

PLAYING CARDS IN A HURRICANE

Lourenco took us out across the harbour in the Zodiac in the drizzle, we climbed up onto Kezia and I set about re-hanging the broken door – it was always going to be me, I knew it and I didn't mind. It was satisfying to be recognised as the one with the mechanical and technical skills and I was pleased to be busy. Using nuts and bolts driven right through the teak door, I secured it back in place on the original hinges, satisfied in the knowledge that the yacht may sink but my door would definitely be in place when it settled on the seabed. Meanwhile, Scouse and Stokie busied themselves, tightening the mooring lines, swabbing and scrubbing the decks. Within the hour, we were ready to head back to shore.

Stokie waved across to Lourenco, he launched the Zodiac from the boatyard's slipway and in seconds, was back alongside Kezia. With practiced ease, we stepped down into the inflatable one by one and once we were seated, Lourenco turned the boat for shore. The sea was choppy even in this protected water behind the high sea wall and the Zodiac was bumping over the wave crests, as we headed for the harbour's stone steps.

And then, faster than I could comprehend, something strange had happened. The sky that was grey, was now a murky green. The afternoon air that was cold and thin, was now cold and thick and it was difficult to breathe it in. I was puzzled to saw rocks covered in seaweed, right over my head.

In that moment, I realised that I was upside down, looking at the seabed and I was blithely inhaling salt sea water with every breath ! Despite the jolt of realisation, I was detached and bemused. How come that I was not aware that I had been catapulted into the water ? Did it happen that fast ?

The thought crossed my mind that I should stop breathing in and head back to the surface. I swivelled upwards and with three strong strokes of my arms and legs, I broke surface. I looked around, treading water and took in the sight of the Zodiac upside down with its smooth, black rubber hull pointing up into the air and Lourenco, Stokie and Scouse all flailing around too. Taking a few seconds to regroup and catch our breath, we swam over to the inflatable and with some effort, managed to turn it back over. Lourenco took hold of the short line attached to its bow and swam away, towing it back into shallow water, by the slipway.

Shocked and disoriented, the three of us reached the stone steps and staggered up to the top, streaming sea water in our wake, as we climbed. Thoroughly soaked and uncertain what to do next, I decided to empty my sea boots. As I bent right down to grasp my right heel and took off the boot, a torrent of sea water gushed out of both my nostrils involuntarily and I stood up sharply in surprise.

'Kezia of Tortola' as we found her, on stilts, in the Nanny Cay boatyard

Kezia, still being worked on by the boatyard's crew, when we arrived from the UK

Scouse making a final inspection of the hull

*All repairs now complete, Kezia was lowered back into the water,
ready for our voyage*

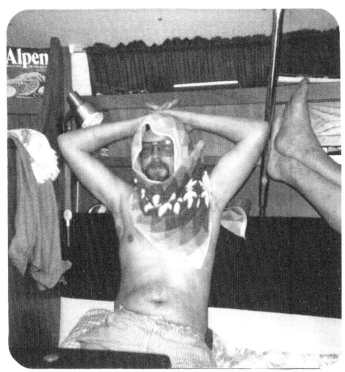

Paul "Scouse" Carswell

The author.. in chef's blues-and-whites

Last view of Tortola

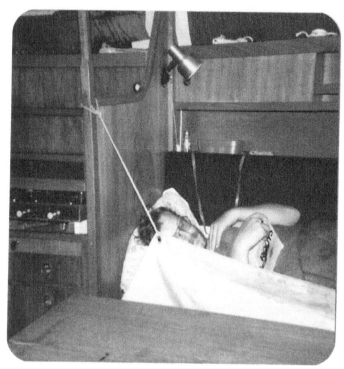

Sleeping arrangements

Oilskins were 'de rigeur' in Mid-Atlantic

No sails up but heeling over

Large bloom of Sargasso weed

ROBERT OLIVER

Mid-Atlantic in heavy seas

100

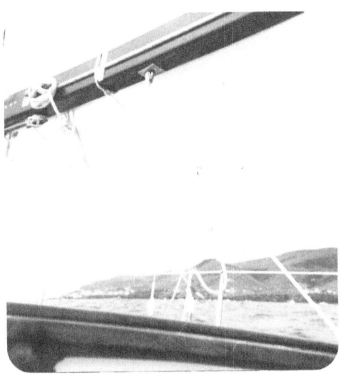

First sight of the Azores after weeks at sea

Safely moored in Santa Cruz, Flores, Azores

Treacherous harbour entrance of Santa Cruz

Sunnier days in Vilamoura

That daring young man on the flying trapeze

More maintenance in Vilamoura

"Frango ! Frango !"

Rock of Gibraltar

Our first glimpse of Sicily

Under tow again, off Mondello

Dodging hydrofoil ferries in the Straits of Messina

Scouse on the quayside at Igoumenitsa

At the wheel for the last miles to Corfu

It didn't hurt and I was thoroughly bemused. So for dramatic effect, I bent forward and once more, another torrent of water streamed out of me. Scouse and Stokie watched me blankly.

'How much water did I take in ?', I wondered. 'At what point, might I have drowned ?'

It occurred me that it was not a painful experience and in all of the long years of my life since that moment, I have never worried about drowning again. There are far worse ways to go.

With that thought, the hard reality of our situation set in. We were cold, wet, soaked and far from home. The afternoon light was failing. We had little option but to head up to the miserable attic room, strip off our clothes and try to dry out.

Whilst we were standing there, dripping and uncertain, Raoul reappeared .

"Hey, come this way ! My friends have offered to help."

Sure enough, several folk had emerged from their cottages and were waving us over to them. An elderly couple were looking and waving at me, so I headed in their direction.

They spoke no English but brought me into their warm parlour, where a coal fire was glowing brightly in the hearth. The old man gently took my jacket from me and hung it dripping over a wooden chair and turned it towards the fire. I left my sea boots by the front door and the old lady led me up the stairs and into an old-fashioned but spotless bathroom. She turned on the hot and cold taps over the large iron bath, put in the plug, turned and placed a large towel into my hands. She smiled at me warmly, leaving the room and shutting the bathroom door behind me. Within minutes, I was immersed in the bath up to my neck, in water as hot as I could stand. As sensation returned to my numb fingers and toes, I felt huge relief and immense gratitude to the kindly old couple that had welcomed this foreign stranger into their home. What would I had done without them ?

Once I had bathed and was drying myself, there was a knock on the bathroom door. When I opened it, I found a large, white dressing gown folded neatly on the floor by the door which I put on. I stepped down into the parlour carrying my wet clothes, trying my best not to drip water on the lino. The lady took them from me and disappeared into the kitchen galley at the rear of the house, presumably to dry them.

She reappeared and smiling again, gestured for me to sit at their small dining table. Her husband sat down to my right and the lady returned, bringing out hot bowls of meat casserole and bread for the three of us. Knowing that they didn't speak any English, I talked to them regardless, pouring out my gratitude and appreciation for the food. The couple smiled and spoke to each other in Portuguese and whilst I did not understand their words, it was clear that they understood how I felt and the sense of what I was saying.

We passed the rest of the evening together, sitting by the fire and drinking tea, listening to the old wooden radio on the sideboard playing classical music. Whilst we hardly spoke, we were completely at ease with each other. At around 11 o'clock, the old lady went out to the kitchen and returned with my clothes in her arms, beaming.

"É bom ! É bom !", she exclaimed.

I touched them and they were indeed, warm and dry ! I smiled in thanks and popped back up to the bathroom and hung the borrowed dressing gown on the back of the door.

In donning my sailing gear again, I felt as If I were in uniform and an alien in the home of this lovely old couple and that it was time for me to take my leave. I went back down the stairs into the parlour and again in English, expressed my sincere thanks for their kindness to me, their lovely meal and for looking after me when I needed it most. With more smiles, handshakes and pats on the back for me, I waved cheerily goodbye and took the few steps back down the cobbled street to our attic room.

When I got into the room, Stokie and Scouse were already back and they had tales of equal kindness.

"What amazing, lovely people they are !" I exclaimed.

Both of them smiled and nodded in agreement. The people of Flores had shown us a generosity of spirit that none of us would ever forget

Next morning, Stokie took his customary daily walk down to our engineer's workshop and to his complete surprise, the morse gear was ready for collection !

As usual, Scouse and I were seated at our regular corner table in the café, drinking very large cups of aromatic coffee as was our wont and watching the world go by. Stokie positively hopped through the door with glee and without a word, carefully placed the morse gear on the table in front of me.

"There you go, Rob", he said. "A present for you !"

I picked up the gleaming piece of machinery and turned it over in my hands. As I inspected it, I realised that whilst the gear handle was the same, the back-plate and the gears that could be clearly seen inside were all brand new. It was so beautifully and precisely made that I was amazed.

"How much did you pay for this ?", I asked him.

"A hundred and thirty escudos. Why, what's wrong with it ?

"Nothing's wrong. It's just that it's a work of art. The guy has hand-crafted every new piece, even the gears themselves. You got an absolute bargain for this standard of workmanship !"

It was clear that we really had benefited from the "make do and mend" attitude of islanders. They had no choice but to machine new replacement parts when they needed them – unable to nip down to a local marine chandlery, the alternative was to wait for manufacturers to air-freight them out to the Azores at an exorbitant price and wait weeks for them to do it, no doubt.

"So... what are you waiting for then, Rob ?" said Stokie with a grin. "Get to it and see if it works !"

I needed no further prompting and with a grin, I got to my feet and left the boys to pay the bill and hurried back down the cobbled street with the precious machinery in both hands. This was our passport out of here. Whilst it had been such a relief to take refuge in Santa Cruz and recuperate amongst these wonderful people, It was time to move on and complete our voyage.

I borrowed a boat and rowed out to the yacht. Refitting the part was very straightforward and it took no more than five minutes to have it bolted back in place in Kezia's cockpit and to reconnect it. With baited breath, I turned the ignition key and pressed the little red start button. The engine started easily but now for the moment of truth - did the gear actually work ?

The yacht was still tied up very securely in her network of ropes but I gently eased the handle forward and I felt a small surge as the gear engaged and the boat began to move. I slipped the morse handle back into neutral, paused and then moved it backwards. As hoped, Kezia began to inch backwards, straining at her ropes. A small cheer went up from the quayside and I looked up to see Stokie and Scouse grinning widely and giving me the thumbs up. I waved back happily, set the gear back to neutral and switched off the engine.

"We're back in business, guys !" I shouted happily across the water.

Less than an hour later, we were back at our regular table in the café.

"So when are we leaving then, boss ?" said Scouse, leaning forward and looking expectantly at Stokie.

"Whoah, hold your horses boy." replied Stokie. "The forecast said Force 8 for the next 48 hours and you know that you don't go out in that unless you have to, especially when we've got to get out of that harbour entrance through those rocks. Also, we have to stock up again on food. Leave it with me, I'll tell you when we're good to go."

And so it went on. For another three days. To Scouse and I, the weather really did not look that bad and it certainly didn't look like Force 8 but Stokie continued to mutter "not yet" and so we waited. I found myself pacing the harbour or looking out over the water from the small bedroom window, eager to be gone. Time and time again, I saw old Ernesto launch a rowing boat and head out to Kezia. When he reached the yacht, he grasped its outside rail that was fitted flush to the deck and checked each rope in turn, tightening and retying them as necessary. He inched his little boat around the yacht by pulling himself (and it) along the outside rail and in this way, managed to go right around Kezia in ten minutes. Satisfied, he rowed back to the boathouse but always returned several hours later, even when the sea was rougher than I would venture out on.

"He cares more about that boat than we do !" I thought to myself.

On the evening of the third day, the three of us got an unexpected invitation to Raoul's house. He welcomed us into a small sitting room with an open coal fire in the hearth, very much like the scene that I had been welcomed into by his neighbours a few days ago and Lourenco was already seated in an armchair in the corner, opposite the fire.

"Welcome, my friends !", he said with a broad smile. "Have you ever tried aguardente velha?" and without waiting for an answer, bustled out of the room to fetch some.

Scouse leaned over to me conspiratorially and whispered gleefully:

"I only speak Spanish but I think he's just offered us a drink of Old Burning Water!"

Within a minute, Lourenco was back with a bottle of pink alcohol and five glasses. He explained that this was rather like our vodka. They fermented it with fruit or other flavourings such as Anis, for as long as possible. It was delicious and it was certainly firewater! Our first sips of the drink resulted in a fit of collective coughing that Raoul and Lourenco found tremendously amusing. Ah, these soft English sailors!

We settled into our drinks, chatted and after a while, Raoul stood up excitedly.

"Come with me – we have something to show you."

He led us into another parlour and gestured towards a tall glass display cabinet with its own internal lighting. As the three of us gathered around him, Raoul picked out a small white ornament and handed it to me with great care. I held it delicately and inspected it. A hand-carved white galleon in impressive, minute detail, complete with masts, full sails and rigging.

"It's very beautiful. I love this detail." I responded. "What is it made from?"

"Whale bone, that we carve by hand." replied Raoul. "It is art I think you call scrimshaw. This has been our hobby for all of us, for many years - sailors do this across the Azores when we are not at sea."

"Is whaling still going on here?" asked Scouse. "It's been banned in most countries."

"It was our main industry here for a hundred years but everything stopped around Flores and Corvo, ten years ago." replied Raoul. "It was a very dangerous thing because in the Azores, we used only open boats and harpoons, not those big ships that the Japanese and Norwegians use."

Open boats? It occurred to me that at least they were giving the whales more than a fighting chance. I thought to ask if they had ever hunted whales themselves but it occurred to me that they must have – old Ernesto was certainly of an age to have done so and so I stayed silent.

I passed the galleon to Stokie and in turn, Raoul handed me more beautifully carved pieces, one by one, none of which was more than four inches long. A dolphin. Two whales. A whale's skeleton perfectly carved in miniature. Various fish, including one that I recognised as a tuna.

We each praised the beauty of the pieces and the brothers beamed with pride.

We said nothing at the time but I sensed the three of us were feeling the same paradox: discomfort with handling items that were products of the whaling industry but marvelling at the beautiful craftsmanship.

In later years, the majority of scrimshaw that I have seen has been scrollwork and engraving on whale teeth. Typically, these have been images of sailing ships or the drama of a whale's capture and killing, carved into the surface but leaving the shape of the bone or tooth intact. What we saw in the brothers' front parlour that evening remains uncommon – the reshaping of the whole bone into a sculpture which to my mind, requires an even greater level of skill and I feel fortunate to have seen it first-hand. Modern scrimshaw is still being produced to this day, on legally-certified whale bones and even hippo or warthog tusks and camel bones.

We returned to the other room and passed a very convivial evening with the brothers. When the bottle was finished, it was time for us to leave.

"And now to our business." said Raoul, putting down his empty glass.

We were slightly puzzled by this sudden pronouncement and looked to each other quizzically. Raoul turned in his seat so he was looking directly into Stokie's face. He had become serious so Stokie turned towards him too.

"Stokie, my friend. When you came to Flores, you were in trouble, this was clear. We were happy to help you and we knew that you would have done the same for us, if we had been in your position. This is what sailors do for each other. But we are very worried about our father. He is not a young man but he is proud and he knows the sea. Every day he is going out to your boat and looking after her, sometimes in very bad weather. His strength is not as it was but he will not stop, even when we tell him it is too much. Lourenco and I worry that something bad will happen very soon because he keeps going out there. Your boat is fixed now and so I ask you this, man to man – for my father's sake – I must ask you to leave Flores."

I was embarrassed and said nothing. I turned to Stokie and waited to see how he would react. Scouse and I knew that he had been prevaricating and delaying for three days and it was now clear that the ruse was up – Raoul and Lourenco knew it too.

"What can I say?", Stokie said quietly. "You have been so good to us and we would never want your father to risk himself for us. We will go – tomorrow - if the weather is good enough."

124

"Thank you, my friend. I am very grateful." said Raoul, rising from his seat. We shook hands with the brothers, said our goodbyes and the cottage door closed quietly behind us in the darkness.

None of us said a word. We had just been run out of town. A few days ago, I was praising the generosity of the people of Santa Cruz but any generosity of spirit had its limits and we had clearly exceeded them.

Day 40 - Sunday, 17th April 1983:

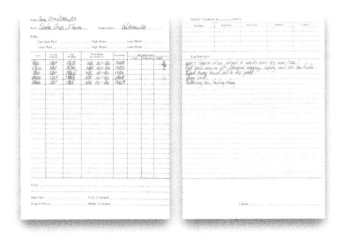

As good as his word, early the next morning, Stokie was galvanised into action. He led us to a small local supermarket to stock-up on our regular sea-faring provisions; canned meat, vegetables and rice. As we were only a week's sailing from mainland Europe, we could take fresh vegetables and fruit which would make a wonderful change but Stokie refused to buy any more food than seven days' worth. "I just hope we don't hit another storm", I thought to myself.

That morning, we made several trips backwards and forwards to Kezia, taking on the food, fresh water and engine diesel. We moved our clothes and meagre provisions out of the attic room and cleaned it as best as we were able.

Finally, by midday, we were ready to leave. We made a quick tour of the town, saying our thank-you's and goodbyes to Alfredo and Maria, to the café and hotel owners, Ernesto and the local people that we had come to know and we boarded the Zodiac for the last time. Raoul and Lourenco ferried us back to Kezia and after we were safely on board, they motored over to the rough harbour outer wall and climbed the steps to where our longer lines were moored. Two of their friends were on hand to help above the harbour steps.

When we were ready to leave, Stokie started the engine and revved it strongly to make sure that it was up to the demands that we were about to make of it. Our exit from the harbour would be less dangerous than our dramatic entrance weeks before but it could go horribly wrong if the engine failed at the wrong moment. With the engine properly warmed, Stokie tested the new morse gear for himself and he too felt the yacht straining on the ropes as I had done, like a thoroughbred horse ready to launch from its starting gate.

He turned to Raoul and Lourenco and shouted:

"Ready to go – cast off!"

This was the starting gun for a frenzy of activity. Scouse and I moved from cleat to cleat on every corner of the yacht, pulling in ropes as they were released by the men around us and tidying them very quickly into neat coils on the deck beside us. Once Stokie was certain that all of these ropes were out of the water and clear of the propeller, he applied full power and pressed the repaired gear lever forward. Kezia surged forward in response and picked up speed as we ran along parallel to the outer harbour wall. Stokie swung the wheel sharply to starboard, heading right towards the boatyard door and then after we had traced an arc taking us safely away from the rock standing as a sentinel over the harbour entrance on our port side, he flung the wheel back the other way so that Kezia's bows were pointing out to sea, right between the two massive rock pillars. As before, the water was foaming and seeming to challenge us to dare to leave. However, Kezia was now moving so strongly and quickly under her own power that there was no stopping her. We powered through the churning water and were steered perfectly between the two rocks. We were out of the harbour and back out into the North Atlantic. We had barely enough time to wave briefly to Raoul and Lourenco as the harbour shrank behind us, such was our motoring speed.

With another dramatic test behind us, we were exhilarated. We were underway again, repaired, refuelled and replenished !

Caught up in the moment, we joined together in a rousing chorus of:

"I am sailing. I am sailing. Home again, 'cross the sea. I am sailing, stormy waters. To be near you, to be free".

Thoroughly trite, corny – but it perfectly summed up our mood !

Chapter Six

Learning to Surf

Day 40 - Sunday, 17th April 1983, 15:00hrs

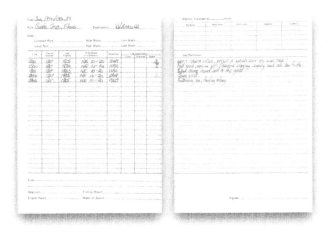

The sky was overcast. A light rain was falling from an overcast sky and the Force 6 wind had stirred the waves into an unpleasant, lumpen mess – a saltwater stew - to greet our first day back at sea for some weeks. After so long on land, my seasickness returned with the pitching and yawing of the yacht. It never ceased to amaze me how a small boat could move in so many different directions in a matter of seconds; up and down, left and right, rolling from one side to the other. Sliding sideways from the crest of the wave was the worst. Add the smell of brine, with the occasional, unexpected lashing of sea water across the face and normally, the misery would be complete.

But not today. Nothing could dampen my high spirits and delight to be back out at sea, finally heading towards our destination again.

At 15:00hrs, well clear of Flores' coast by now and into open water, Stokie switched off the engine and Scouse and I swarmed over the deck, removing the canvas sail sleeve that had been protecting the mainsail and winding the ropes around the winches ready for action. Despite our enthusiasm to get under way, we carefully checked each part of the rigging, looking for missing or frayed parts, even down to the safety rail that went completely around the yacht. As I was carefully squeezing each inch of the plastic-coated white cable between my fingers checking for breakages, something caught my eye and I looked up to see a huge green turtle swimming imperiously past me, gently paddling its flippers through the water. I called the others to my side and we laughed at the haughty demeanour of this old sea giant.

He didn't pause for one moment or break stroke and soon was gone.

As Scouse and I were hoisting the mainsail and the jib, the wind changed round to the north-east, which was all to the good and within seconds, both sails were full and Kezia began to move under her own power again.

Stokie adjusted our course slightly and it dawned upon us that not only was the wind in a perfect direction but we had a following sea. The waves were perfectly lined up directly behind us and for the first time in 1,800 miles, I experienced the strange feeling of surfing in a yacht. Undoubtedly, most of our speed and power was coming from the favourable wind and our sails but every few seconds, the yacht was picked up slightly and we felt a surge as we were launched forward, noticeably faster. Then the feeling subsided, Kezia slowed and then settled deeper in the water. Suddenly, another short surge would happen as a new wave lifted and then passed under us.

I looked back to where Stokie was standing still behind the wheel. He was beaming broadly.

"Miles make smiles ! And smiles are beer miles !" he exclaims.

Not exactly Samuel Taylor Coleridge but we smiled and shared his enthusiasm for our newfound speed for home.

This exhilarating combination of perfect winds and a following sea carried on long after dark and we sat together in the cockpit until 10pm, enjoying this long moment.

I awoke at 4am for my next watch, swung my legs out of my bunk and begin to pull on my wet gear and boots. Within seconds, I was back out on deck in the cool, salt sea air. Cutting through the darkness, I saw the flash of a lighthouse beam, only a few miles away to the north.

"Where are we ?" I asked Scouse.

"Off Faial, apparently" he said.

"God, think how long it's taken to get here. Can you imagine what it would had been like if we had decided to press on that morning in Flores ?"

"Yeah, we'd have been eating each other by now !" he grinned.

Over the next five hours, we passed the islands of Sao Jorge and Grasciosa. The latter was not a welcome sight. It meant we were off course, so we swung thirty degrees east and soon, all was well again. In the channels between the islands, there was a distinct funnel effect and we experienced that wonderful, disconcerting surfing effect, as we passed them by.

At 8pm that evening, we were caught by a sudden squall which exploded upon us and we worked quickly to reef the mainsail and roll the jib in. Within four minutes, we had everything under control again and we continued to sail very quickly, albeit a little more cautiously. Perhaps our desire to get on and get home was causing us to be a little too 'gung-ho' in our decision making?

That new caution was well-founded because later in the early hours of the next day, we were forced to stop sailing altogether for two hours and wait for that weather front to pass through. We started off again, sailing well for five hours before another sudden squall hit and with a large and ominous tearing sound, the jib tore right along its foot as if it were a thin, cotton bed-sheet. If the weather carried on like this, we would run out of sails soon.

Fortunately, on inspecting the damage, Scouse realised that despite the ominous ripping sound, the jib had only torn along its backing so it could still be used – but carefully.

This pattern of wonderful, fast sailing, punctuated by the frenzied activity caused by a sudden squall, carried on right through the night and none of us got much sleep, whether 'on watch' or off. We sighted the island of Sao Miguel, approximately 30 miles away, 125° eastwards and shortly after, we left the last of the Azores behind us. We were now 200 miles away from Flores and surging towards the south-western coast of Portugal - and mainland Europe.

Day 43 - Wednesday, 20th April 1983, 00:30hrs:

Yet again, sailing had become impossible because of new, strong gusts that were stretching our fragile sails to breaking point and a heavy swell that was causing us to roll sideways from the crests of the waves. Consequently, we made little progress. Finally, we pointed Kezia into wind, took down the largest sails and "lay a hull", resigned to sitting out this exasperating, changeable weather until morning.

First light revealed blue skies, flatter seas, sunshine and a kinder wind. By 07:30hrs all of our sails were aloft again and we were flying . My 15:00hrs entry in the yacht log read:

"Best watch, this leg."

And at midnight:

"Doubled our watches again but making up for it in beer knots !"

Our tremendous progress was taking us towards the nearest bar.

By 2am, the sea was flattening and Kezia was flying through the night at top speed. Beneath my hands at the wheel, I felt the truly wonderful, exhilarating sensation as her hull lifted once again and she began to plane across the surface in the darkness, barely kissing the water. Her rigging was singing with a low hum as every cable, rope and sail was stretched to the maximum, vibrating gently and working hard. The salt sea air was no longer bitterly cold and there was a much-welcome warmth, long after the sun had set.

By mid-morning the next day, the wind and waves had swung around behind us. All three of us spent most of the day on deck, experimenting with different sail combinations that allowed us to hoist the maximum amount of sail area. Normally, well-equipped yachts have a spinnaker to achieve this – a large voluminous sail that stretches up and forward in front of a yacht and dramatically increases its speed. Loving her as we might, we couldn't describe Kezia as a well-equipped yacht. She had no spinnaker and so we had to improvise as best we could. We put one jib sail out to the left on a pole, with its rope tied back to one winch in the cockpit. Then, in a perfectly-symmetrical arrangement, we hoisted the other jib sail out to the right on a pole and tied this back to the winch on the right of the cockpit. The one snag with this arrangement was that if we ran into a sudden squall, it took precious minutes to take down these contraptions which wasn't good and was bordering on the downright dangerous. In extreme conditions, with too much sail and a following sea and wind, boats can "pitch-pole" – the stern comes up, the bow digs into the water and whole yacht somersaults – generally only once but fatally. Five years later, I was to execute this same pitch-pole manoeuvre perfectly. Thankfully, I was in a 12' long Laser dinghy and only resulted in my being catapulted headlong into the water at great speed but in relative safety.

However, we were still 300 miles from mainland Europe and in a degree of danger by taking this risk. That said, we had become very experienced, Stokie was steering the yacht with total concentration whilst we watched the wind and waves for any sign of change. We were so determined to make "beer miles" that we were happy to take the risk – and it was tremendously good fun, surfing in a yacht.

Day 46 - Saturday 23rd April, 1983:

Three days passed in this way. Occasionally, a squall charged through and we had to take down our complicated "goose wing" contraption down in good time and let it pass, occasionally having to stop completely if the conditions were severe enough. This could happen at any time of the day or night and I was regularly wakened from a deep sleep, warm in my bunk, by a shout of:

"All hands on deck. Any time in the next 30 seconds will do, thanks."

That day was probably our best sailing day so far. Again, blue skies, warm air, a strong following wind and high, surging waves right behind, powering us forward. As had become normal now, we put up our "goose-wing" jib sails in our well-practiced routine and enjoyed the ride.

But something had changed and I became increasingly uneasy. This was becoming less enjoyable and we seemed to have been sailing so hard, for so long, it seemed inevitable that something would go wrong. I looked to Scouse and Stokie for any sign that they felt it too but they seemed oblivious, so I said nothing.

The wind continued to pick up but the squalls were less frequent so we sailed on, hour after hour. Stokie had been at the wheel for almost five hours now without a break which was very unusual, considering our normal "three hours on" rule in daylight hours.

"Do you want me to take over, Stokie ?" I asked. "You've been steering for hours, you must be done in."

"Thanks but I'd better do this." he said, "We are dancing on a bit of tightrope here. We are going so fast and with the sea the way it is, right behind us, if I veer off 10 degrees, she will be knocked down on her side. Not good. "Miles make smiles" though!"

So, he steered right through the day and as new gusts of winds struck us from behind and our sails stretched and strained to breaking point in front of us, Scouse laughed and suddenly burst out:

"I've thought of a new motto for us. 'The Kezia Kamikaze Crew' sail on through!"

We laughed at the exhilarating madness of what we were doing. It didn't last much longer. As darkness fell, we lost our collective nerve, took down the goose-winged sails and settled in for a quieter night. Stokie retired to his bunk after we had eaten, exhausted by the long hours of intense concentration.

My last log entry of the day at 10pm read:

"A fine, moonlicht nicht."

At the wheel alone in the darkness, I started to pick out the navigation lights of distant ships around us for the first time. Our long, lonely days in mid-ocean were coming to an end. We had company.

Chapter Seven

Home from Home

Day 49 - Tuesday 26th April 1983, 13:00hrs:

Standing on the new wooden pontoon of Vilamoura marina, I felt a huge sense of relief. This was what I had imagined a suitable port to be like before we had been forced to make our emergency stop in the Azores. The presence of so many white 8 to 10 metre yachts around me, very much like our Kezia, was tremendously reassuring. I saw small shops and bars lining the northern edge of the marina. Over my shoulder, near the harbour entrance, was a small boatyard with an engineering workshop of the type that we had only dreamed of during our long sojourn in Flores, with a refuelling pump within easy reach on the quayside. There was a water tap on a nearby metal girder that the floating pontoon was secured to. A yachtsman was walking down the wooden ramp from the quayside to his yacht, nonchalantly carrying a cardboard box of groceries.

"Try doing that in Flores !", I thought to myself.

The next two weeks passed in a very enjoyable, yet unremarkable routine of carrying out yet more repairs to the yacht during the days and then quiet evenings out together in local bars or cafés. The work included those difficult tasks that we had been putting off, such as investigating the source of the contaminated water problem which involved undoing a considerable amount of screws and lifting the fibreglass lids off the tanks. I was disappointed not to find anything obvious. No dead rodents or cockroaches, no film of oil on the water, just that same, strange fibreglass smell that had been tainting our water for weeks. The old tanks were making the water stale and unpleasant but it wasn't dangerous or unfit to drink. I cleaned them out thoroughly and sealed them up again tightly.

After three days, David Blackwell arrived on another yacht that he was delivering elsewhere, with his own crew. With the difficulties in the Azores behind them, Stokie and David were on excellent terms again and we spent two nights out on the town with them.

A particular highlight was a walk into Quarteira, the old town, no more than a half-mile away to the north-east over rough scrub ground.

"I remember a really great chicken restaurant in town." said David. "Everyone like chicken? Great, we're off then." he said without further debate.

The six of us picked our way over the mounds of broken bricks and rubble that lay between the marina and Quarteira – this would be replaced with a hotel and casino by the time that I returned 25 years later. We wandered the back streets of the town for half an hour fruitlessly trying to find this famed restaurant and when we finally arrived, Stokie, Scouse and I understood why it was so difficult.

The "restaurant" was actually a large outhouse under a corrugated concrete roof, marked only with a shuttered garage entrance door which was flung upwards during opening hours. Along the back wall was a line of steel drums which were filled with glowing charcoal and on which, countless chicken pieces were cooking and giving off a truly delicious smell.

It was fitted out like a canteen. Long rows of trestle tables and bench seats ran from one side to the other and the room was large enough to have three sets of these. The one concession to comfort (and colour) was the red floral, vinyl tablecloth – one long, continuous expanse from one end to the other, on every table.

Many areas of the tables were already filled with families and group of friends and we were expected to fit in - which we did with pleasure. The service was friendly but basic. Fresh bread was brought to us in small baskets as soon as we were settled and the only drinks available were red wine or beer. The food on offer was barbecued chicken with chips and salad.

It was magnificent. It was simply cooked but imbued with that smoky, barbecued flavour that I have been able to recall and savour, over decades.

I found out many years later that the restaurant was famed far and wide and rightly so. Its name ? "Frango ! Frango !" or in English, "Chicken ! Chicken !". It could not had been more aptly named.

On the way back to the marina in the darkness, we lost our way crossing the wasteland between Quarteira and Vilamoura and found our way barred by a 12-foot-high chain-link fence for many yards in both directions. Our little group cursed, shrugged and started to trudge along the fence to round it. However, fuelled by several Portuguese beers, I refused to admit defeat. I reached up and took held of the chain links above my head and then swiftly climbed the fence, using my hands to pull me up, as my feet used the lower links for footholds. Within seconds, I was astride the top of the fence and then started a careful but quick descent to the ground. I had to wait for another two minutes before the rest of the group appeared out of the dark and we rejoined the path home.

"That looked way too much effort, mate !" grinned Scouse. "Bloody youngsters." added Stokie.

Little did I realise that in performing this little demonstration, I was setting myself up to repeat this same feat in much more dangerous circumstances, later in Sicily.

For the second time in a month, I couldn't understand why we were holding out in a foreign port. The danger had receded, Kezia was basically sea-worthy (at long last) and we had everything we needed to set sail and finish our voyage. Stokie was clearly unworried, even jovial – so perhaps we were on holiday. Scouse and I held our tongues this time. For once, we had enough food and enough money for beer and cigarettes, it was warm and sunny and we knew that we would leave in good time.

And sure enough, one day, he announced that we would be leaving the next day so perhaps the runes were right, the tea leaves had been read and the planets had aligned.

PLAYING CARDS IN A HURRICANE

Day 58 - Thursday, 5th May 1983, 09:45hrs:

With Scouse at the stern and myself on the bow, we untied our ropes from the stanchions on the pontoon, gave Kezia a gentle shove sideways away from the side and jumped the widening gap onto the yacht at either end. Stokie powered up the diesel engine and we carefully threaded our way through yachts and pontoons to the harbour entrance. Once safely through, we unfurled the mainsail and the jib. Within minutes, we had the sails up and stretched to their full extent in a gentle 15 knot south-easterly wind. With the motor on and all our sails aloft, we passed quickly along the coast of the Algarve and within two hours, were sailing past Faro airport.

It was warm and overcast. For the first time, I felt that we were cruising like day trippers, rather than professional sailors. After the rigours of the North Atlantic, the entrance to the Mediterranean seemed rather like a boating lake to me, although there was a noticeable increase in the amount of big ships around us, so our safety was only relative. By 22:00hrs, we were off Cadiz and sailing strongly eastwards into a warm, quiet night.

In the early hours, we passed by Cape Trafalgar and by 04:00hrs, I could see Cape Espartel in North Africa to the south but we were too busy to enjoy it – the volume of shipping was very heavy and we had to keep our wits literally about us. Our watches were dominated not by the rigours of sailing but monitoring what each and every ship around us was doing: what direction it was heading and at what speed. Which one was potentially trying to run us down now?

As dawn broke, we rounded the promontory of Califa and there was the Rock of Gibraltar in front of us, its limestone cliffs gleaming in the early May morning sun.

It is difficult to describe Gibraltar if you have not seen it with your own eyes. It stands out into the sea on a peninsular that is less than 2.5 square miles. Most of that is dominated by the Rock itself, so what little usable building land that there is, is crammed with apartment buildings, houses, hotels and office blocks – but only in the middle. The north side of the island is taken up by the airport with its runway that crosses the island and forms the land border with La Línea de la Concepción, the Spanish town on the other side of the chain-link fence. The south side, facing out to sea, is dominated by imposing military buildings. In summary, it looks like the fortress that it is, dominating the landscape, imposing and impressive.

Stokie had been here many times and we took a straight line up the western bay and without any hesitation, sailed straight into the small marina near to the airport. We moored up in the smaller, heavily concreted marina and within 30 minutes had secured Kezia and were eager to see the sights of Gibraltar.

There was something eerily reminiscent about Gibraltar. Imagine walking in a foreign land, under a tropical sun, in a thoroughly unfamiliar landscape. However, there are traditional, red English telephone boxes and letter boxes on every corner. There are pubs with names such as the Red Lion and the Wembley bar. Cars are driving on the left and the shops around you are named Marks & Spencer, Mothercare, Tesco, BHS and Dorothy Perkins.

The three of us wandered through the back streets of Gibraltar, taking in the sights with growing smiles upon our faces. On Main Street, we had covered less than 100 yards before a traditional-looking pub named "The Angry Friar" standing on a corner, beckoned to us. We stepped through its dark entrance and were instantly transported back home. Everything about this old pub was authentic and English. There was a long oak

147

bar lined with beer taps behind the counter, drip mats on the tables, the floor was covered with a red tapestried carpet that had seen many cigarette ends and better days. One wall was dominated by a glass-fronted display case that contained all manner of memorabilia from Old Blighty – old matchbox cars, silver statuettes of knights and a dazzling array of silver and chrome cigarette lighters with a prominent sign emblazoned across its footing saying "Do Not Touch" in angry red letters.

"What's it going to be then, lads ?" said Scouse with a grin.

"It's gotta be best bitter after coming all this way !", I exclaimed.

Within two minutes, each of us had a traditional glass tankard in his hand, filled with best bitter.

"To us !" said Stokie with a flourish. "Let's hope it's been worth the journey !"

It was probably no more than keg bitter but to us, it tasted magical after more than three months away from home. At first sip, the rich, bitter flavour of hops and yeast cancelled out all the horrors of Budweiser and American light beers in an instant.

"Feels like home from home here", I said.

The others grinned and said nothing. They were too busy drawing deeply on their pints.

Our visit to Gibraltar was fleeting. Apart from the long afternoon taking in the sights (several traditional English pubs actually), our activities the next morning centred around food shopping at a small supermarket near the marina. By Stokie's estimation, we had only another week's sailing and then we would be in Corfu, at journey's end and for that reason, refused to buy anything other than basic provisions. We walked the bags of food back down the concrete walkway of the marina and deposited them in Kezia's galley.

I was seething and exasperated – we were back on starvation rations again.

"Stokie, I'm nipping back into town. Need to get one or two things for myself. Scouse – fancy a walk?"

As we headed back along the harbour wall, Scouse looked at me quizzically.

"What are we doin' then ? You look like a man with a plan !"

"Well, if he won't feed us, there's no reason for us to starve, we've got David's money still."

We headed back to the supermarket and this time, we bought what we really needed and indeed what we fancied too. Deciding that Stokie had at least provisioned our main meal every day, we bought copious amounts of bacon, eggs, fresh fruit, baked beans, biscuits, bread, jam, tea, coffee, milk, chocolate and cigarettes. No alcohol 'though because that was an accepted rule on board. We headed back to the marina, both of us with our own cardboard box filled to the brim with our extra rations. As we passed these over Kezia's railing to each other and took them down to the saloon, I noticed Stokie looking on ruefully and said nothing. I knew it was petty but I was angry about the way that he had cut our rations to save his money. I would not let this happen again.

Chapter Eight

Fire !

Day 60 - Saturday 7th May 1983, 12:00hrs

At midday, we slipped out of Gibraltar's marina in our now practiced way and headed out into the western bay. We turned south towards the open water of the Mediterranean and although we made progress, it was painfully laborious. We were alternately becalmed or doing seven knots and this pattern repeated itself many times. The heat had caused the horizon to soften and ultimately it disappeared into an attractive white wispy haze with the sun shining brightly above us. After playing with various sails in different configurations for three hours with little effect, we switched the engine on and motored, letting the yards of canvas flap amateurishly as we went. By 22:00hrs, the wind had moved around to the south-west and was stronger. We were able to put up our goose-winged jib sails again in the twilight and made better progress.

By the next morning, the haze had cleared completely and we were sailing directly eastwards in fine weather and beautiful sunshine. All three of us were on deck at 07:00hrs and sitting on the port side of the cockpit, I had the wonderful surprise of seeing a shark's dorsal fin coursing directly towards us from the opposite direction. It barely wavered as it passed from stem to stern in seconds less than six feet away from me as it flashed by. I marvelled at the sculpted beauty of the steel grey, glistening fin as it sliced the water and kept on going until it was lost in the distance westwards, well behind the yacht. He was heading for the open water of the Atlantic and would be there within hours.

After two hours, Stokie and Scouse retired to their bunks. It was my watch and we were settling into our normal sailing routine so with nothing for them to do, they went below to rest.

In perfect weather with light fair-weather clouds dotting the sky, I sailed happily on. The yacht was beautifully set-up and I was happy to be left alone for the next hour.

Staring intently forward, my attention was caught by a black object, thousands of feet up in the sky which seconds before I had noted moving steadily northwards. To my great surprise, it tumbled down suddenly in an erratic dive from its great height, seemingly out of control. Assuming that it must be an aircraft, I watched with horror, anticipating that within seconds it would fall into the sea as it was now only a very small distance above the water. I watched for the impact and spout of water that never came.

Now, I was even more confused because I could see the black dot silhouetted against a low, white cloud on the horizon but it appeared to be completely stationary, hovering close to the sea.

I watched fascinated – was it an illusion or was the black dot growing in size as I watched ? Slowly, the truth dawned upon me, my stomach began to knot and I felt my body tense in anticipation. Inexorably, the black dot got bigger and bigger, altered course and began to bear down on us.

I could have called out to Stokie and Scouse to warn them but what would be the point ? It was nearly upon us now, having covered several miles of water in a matter of seconds.

In those last seconds, I shut my eyes and steeled myself for what I knew was to come. There was an earth- shattering scream as 30 tons of blue and grey steel hurtled over Kezia's mast at 500 miles per hour. I could see it coming but I felt as if my insides had been liquefied by the noise and the shockwave that it left behind.

"WHAT THE... ?"

I heard Scouse and Stokie screaming profanities below, along with banging and scuffling sounds as they hit their heads on the fibreglass roof in shock.

I looked back over my shoulder and saw the Blackburn Buccaneer jet perform a victory roll in salute to me as it gained height and disappeared towards the RAF base on Gibraltar.

"Settle down, chaps." I shouted down to them gleefully, as the noise subsided.

"It was just the RAF dropping in to say 'Hello' to us from 5,000 feet !"

PLAYING CARDS IN A HURRICANE

Day 62 - Monday 9th May 1983, 02:00hrs

The Mediterranean wind was a fickle creature. Late last night, it was a case of "All hands on deck !" as a sudden squall caught us with all of our sails aloft and Kezia launched forward at great speed. And still the wind kept on rising to the point that our starboard rail was underwater and the yacht was being pushed flat onto her side, as if by an unseen hand. Stokie bellowed for help and we crashed up onto the deck barefoot and in our underwear, such was the urgency in his call. Within seconds, we loosened the ropes tied up on the winches, Kezia's breakneck speed eased a little and she was able to come upright. Emergency over.

Now, four hours later, the wind had hushed itself and we were becalmed, no longer moving. Once again, the sails filled with wind, then emptied themselves just as quickly and flapped list-lessly in the heat of the night. The right thing to do would be to prime the engine, switch the electrics on and start the engine but I was feeling quietly rebellious and felt like taking it easy.

I fetched my Sony Walkman from down below and slotted Roxy Music's latest album "Flesh and Blood" into it and switched it on. I had bought it in Worcester just before coming away on this trip and I was immensely proud of it. For the first time, music had become truly portable in this grey shiny little device, hardly bigger than a music cassette itself and its sound quality was like nothing I had heard before.

I stretched out on the fibreglass deck near the mainmast and looked directly up at the stars. As I watched and my eyes become trained to them, the several hundred stars that one can never normally see on land turned into thousands and then millions, visible to the naked eye as miniscule pin-pricks of light. I could see the white blur of the Milky Way stretching up diagonally across my field of view and the whole sight was truly breath-tak-ing. In the years to come, the only time that I was ever able to see the stars with such clarity again, was on a night safari in the Kruger National Park in South Africa, where there was no light pollution either.

I passed my night-watch in this way, feeding a new tape into the Walkman as each album ended, full of wonderment at the blissful combination of music, the warm night air and the stars. I managed to keep adequate watch around me for shipping, having never forgotten the fright caused by Scouse's lapse of concentration in the middle of the storm in mid-Atlantic, weeks earlier. As the end of my shift approached, I returned the Walkman to the shelves above my bunk and got back the wheel.

"Stokie – 10 minutes!" I shouted.

At 04:00hrs, exactly on time, he surfaced through his aft cabin hatch blearily.

"What's happening? Seems quiet."

"Wind's completely dropped in the last 20 minutes." I lied happily. "Can we put the engine on?"

"Sure! Give me a hand with it and you can turn in for bed."

Within minutes, with the diesel engine clattering noisily in its compartment under the saloon table by my bunk, I slipped immediately into a contented and relaxed sleep almost immediately. What a wonderful, memorable night that was!

In the four days since leaving Gibraltar, we had been motoring for 30 hours, which was poor for a sailing vessel. The north-westerly wind continued to blow at no more than 10 knots so eventually, we took the sails down because the continual slapping noise had become intensely irritating. Then, what little wind there was swung around to east-south-east – right on our nose, in the direction that we were heading. What else could go wrong?

"Time for tea, boys !" I announced.

To keep myself busy, I took tea and coffee orders and headed down to the galley and put the kettle on the gas stove.

The engine was operating normally behind me, its din barely tolerable in that confined space. I was standing by the stove, spooning coffee granules into one cup and placing a tea-bag in the other when I heard a loud pop and then a thoroughly-unusual sound, like wind rushing through a hole.

I looked to my left and the fuse-box that was sited right under the stairs to the cockpit was ablaze and blue smoke was gushing horizontally out of its side vents in strong jets. Flames were shooting up and out of these slots and becoming stronger as I watched.

Bizarrely, Stokie and Scouse were seated behind the wheel and were chatting normally. They had not seen what was going on below yet I could see them through the smoke. Equally strangely, the engine seemed unperturbed either and was clattering away normally.

"Fire ! Fire !" I shouted, managing to sound both panicked and angry at the same time.

My crewmates jumped to their feet in alarm and Stokie reached down in that instant and switched off the engine. It made no difference – the flames and plumes of smoke were still pouring out of the box.

My first instinct was to vault up and over the flames and escape out into the fresh air. Get out while you can!

In that same instant, an inner voice spoke to me, "So - you escape out onto the deck and what then? When the fire takes hold, you will all be swimming the Mediterranean within half-an-hour. Stay and fight it!"

I soaked a tea towel under the tap and wrapped it tightly around my hand. I took up a long-handled knife and thrusting it into the hot smoke, managed to get the tip of the knife into the edge of the wooden plywood cover on the front of the fuse-box and with a sharp flick, managed to dislodge it. It fell with a clatter onto the floor behind the stairs, still smoking.

Now, I was frightened. The newly-exposed fire leaped up and outwards, feeding on the fresh air that I had just exposed it to.

159

I reached to my right and pulled down a small, red fire extinguisher from the racking, high up on the bulkhead of the galley. I pulled out the retaining split-pin and squeezed the handle, directing a powerful white cloud of carbon dioxide at the seat of the fire. Within ten seconds, the raging fire in the fuse-box was put out and I turned my attention to the smoking cover at my feet. For the next couple of minutes, I watched for any sign of glowing embers, making sure that everything was finished, giving them an occasional blast from the extinguisher to be certain.

Finally, I turned towards Stokie and Scouse jubilantly raising the extinguisher to them:

"Hey, I found something that actually works on this crappy boat!"

"Yeah, very good, Rob." said Stokie. "But what caused it? I need to know – have a good look over it when it's cooled down."

To give it time to do that, I climbed up onto the deck and enjoyed the fresh air. There was much sighing and smiling at our closest call to date.

"Thought we were all going for a swim a moment ago!" blurted Scouse.

"I wouldn't want to do that again." said Stokie. "I've been ship-wrecked on a yacht once before and it's no fun when you can't swim."

"What do you mean, when was that ?" asks Scouse incredulous-ly.

"And what do you mean, you can't swim ?" I said. "You've been on boats for years !"

While we waited for the fuse-box to cool down, Stokie told us his story:

"I was doing a yacht delivery with David in the Red Sea and it was thick fog that night. We could hear big ships moving around us and there were a lot of foghorns going but it was impossible to tell where anything was because the sound behaves weirdly in those conditions. Anyway, I was on the tip of the bow, looking out and David was at the other end, on the stern. Suddenly, before we could do anything about it, the bow of a supertanker appeared out of the fog towering above us and it just chopped us in half and kept going.

"It literally passed between David and me – about 40,000 tons of it. It smashed the boat to pieces beneath our feet and next, we were floating in the Red Sea surrounded by fibreglass and debris. I grabbed a seat cushion for buoyancy because I couldn't swim. David was great. He kept me from panicking about it and

I realised that I could float. We were left in the water for hours and we kept each other alive, just talking, taking the piss out each other, laughing at the madness of having survived being run over by an oil tanker.

"Eventually, the fog burned away and we were floating around in the water for the whole of the following night and the day after. The worst thing was the fear of sharks. The Red Sea was one of the most shark-infested waters in the world and we got obsessed, afraid to even piss in the water in case it attracted them. Suddenly, out of the blue, David said:

"Do you know, we are only two miles from land ?"

"What ? Even I could swim that !" I replied.

"What, straight down ?" said David with an evil grin.

"We wouldn't have survived another night. We were sunburned, exhausted and dehydrated and we had nothing left.

"Ships had been passing us all the time but no-one had even seen us. They weren't looking for us because the tanker that got us hadn't even noticed that it had hit something.

"In the end, a crewman standing at the rail of one of these ships saw my red jacket in the water and sounded the alarm. The ship stopped and they launched a boat for us. If it hadn't been for my red jacket, we'd both be dead now.

"So... I'm very, very pleased that I don't have to do that again tonight!"

Scouse and I were stunned that anyone could survive being run down by a ship and float in shark-infested waters for a couple of days. Suddenly, I felt as if we had a lucky talisman with us. If Stokie could survive that, sailing the last bit of the Med should be literally a breeze!

At this, I went back down below to the fuse-box and started to pick through the blackened connections to try and figure out what had happened. I was much relieved to find that despite all the flames, the fuse-box was still working and making the right connections. I tested the navigation lights, the compass light, the interior cabin lights, the radio – everything was fine, everything worked. It was the plywood casing that gave fuel to the fire and was badly charred. I wasn't in the least worried about that as it could be replaced by someone else once we reached Corfu.

"Add *that* to the list!" I said to myself.

And so finally, working methodically through the fuse-box, I found the source of the fire. A strange, unrecognisable black cigar-shaped object had fused diagonally across several contacts, creating a short-circuit and causing the resulting fire. I selected a pair of long-jawed pliers and delicately extricated it from the box.

I held the object aloft in the pliers and called out to Stokie and Scouse who were sitting and chatting in the cockpit.

"Here it is. Here is the culprit." I called to them.

"What the hell is that ?" replied Stokie, thoroughly baffled.

"The biggest, fattest, dead-est cockroach you ever did see !" I said triumphantly.

Chapter Nine

Thieves in the Night

Day 65 - Thursday 12th May 1983, 09:00hrs

Last night, we had enjoyed a favourable swell with Kezia riding the wave crests, accelerated by a following wind and powering along strongly under sullen skies. We had been exhilarated by the progress we were making and we felt that the remaining miles were ticking away before our eyes.

However, this new-found speed was stolen away from us by daybreak as the wind dropped to 5 knots. Worse still, we found ourselves on the same route as a white cruise liner, heading East. Even at a distance, its size was daunting and no matter what course alteration we made to escape it, it seemed to be getting inexorably closer as if she was hunting us. Frustrated by the fruitlessness of our attempts to escape, Stokie decided to made a decisive turn and then motor away. He ordered us to furl the jib sail, which was quickly done and we prepared to turn to starboard and hopefully, safety.

Scouse and I returned to the cockpit as he checked that the throttle was in neutral and turned the key as a precursor to pressing the ignition switch. There was an ominous silence where there should have been the high-pitched tone as the key was turned, immediately before an engine start. He pressed the ignition button repeatedly but there was nothing, apart from a click.

"Either the battery is flat, which doesn't make sense as we had the engine running for hours yesterday, or we've got another damned electrical problem." I said. Stokie nodded and decided: "No time to screw around with that now, we'll sail south and get out of the way of that liner. Get the jib out again." Scouse stepped up, unlocked the line from its stopping block and looped it around the winch. Wordlessly, he wound quickly and urgently and the jib began to unroll quickly. It filled with wind, went taught and we felt the boat surge forward, albeit not in a direction that helped us towards the Messina Straits between Sicily and Italy.

Five minutes later, the cruise liner had overtaken us and was powering eastwards, so we went about and headed North East to pick up our original course.

"We just couldn't catch a break, could we ?" said Scouse and we all nodded in agreement. "Just when we thought we were winning, she lets us down again."

"Just like every other woman in my life !" announced Stokie.

I set to work, checking the battery and wiring connections and retried the engine. Everything was dead. We had no power whatsoever, not even for navigation lights at night. We weren't particularly surprised or downhearted. We had come to expect these problems and believed that nothing could be as dangerous as floating near the Azores at night, powerless, in bad weather and wallowing seas. The Mediterranean seemed less threatening, the sea was calm, we were under blue skies and a blazing sun. So we sailed on towards the north coast of Sicily.

We spent the next three days tacking backwards and forwards past the Aegadian Islands in Italian territorial waters, west of Sicily, as the wind had swung right around to the East, right on our nose. The wind dropped to less than 5 knots and we felt that we were making little headway, although there was a current that helped us as we threaded between the islands. We were achieving less than 100 miles each day as we dawdled along in this way.

Day 68 - Sunday 15th May 1983, 00:00hrs

From midnight, we were becalmed for all of our two-hour watches, the sails hanging limply down but at other times, a gentle wind resumed and we made a little progress. In this way, we covered 26 miles by midday and found ourselves drifting aimlessly one mile off the port of Mondello, on the northern coast of Sicily. Behind the port, the major city of Palermo lay due south.

This was immensely frustrating for us, knowing that with a working motor, we could be in the port within minutes, mooring up and then going in search of a Sicilian lunch and a cooling beer. Meanwhile, we drifted silently, under a merciless midday sun.

An hour later, we noticed a large yacht motoring up behind us on the same course and eventually it slowed and pulled alongside - a gleaming white, modern 40-foot vessel called 'Pichincha II' under a Swiss flag. "Are you broken down ? Would you like a tow ?" the skipper called across to us. "Yes please !" we called back enthusiastically, all smiles. They threw us a line from their stern, which Scouse tied to a cleat on our bow and we were finally underway towards Mondello.

In less than 20 minutes, we were moored in a small marina, stern first against the harbour wall which was built from very thick, block concrete. It looked like a remnant from World War II but our relief at reaching dry land overrode any aesthetic concerns about our surroundings. We offered our sincere thanks to the other crew who waved us away with smiles. The Swiss yacht stayed briefly for lunch and then motored away in an easy, effortless manner. We looked on enviously, marooned again and facing more repairs before we could even think of continuing our journey - we needed both our electrics and our engine working for safety and comfort.

———✈———

Stokie climbed off the boat, walked across the quay, through a wide-flung, open gate in a tall chain link fence to a large steel-panelled workshop inside a compound. Its main shutter was rolled up and within it, we could see six yachts on stands, without their masts, evenly spaced and in different stages of repair or re-spraying. No-one could be seen anywhere but Stokie turned towards what looked like a small office on the left within the vaulted workshop and disappeared inside. After several minutes, he emerged with a figure in blue overalls and they walked a beeline towards us. They reached Kezia and wordlessly stepped onboard and down into the cockpit. Stokie didn't introduce the workman and he looked even less likely to introduce himself but I observed him silently. Of medium height, middle-aged but thin, skin darkened and wizened by years in the sunlight, he looked like he meant business. Humourless, intense and already focusing his gaze on the morse gear, the electrical wiring and then the engine, he visited each in turn, removing covers and trying switches and the ignition key. I was relieved when he tried to start the engine and failed. It would have been deeply embarrassing for me if it was to start immediately and a poor reflection of my engine management skills.

"Not good. Electrics broken." said the mechanic suddenly in good but heavily accented English.

"What's the problem ?" said Stokie. "Any idea what's wrong ?"

"I do not know. Perhaps battery, perhaps fuse but I can fix it, for sure."

"Please can you work on it today ? We need to get to Corfu soon." said Stokie.

"Sure, no problem, I do it now."

"Well, any idea how much it will cost ?"

"If it is simple, like battery and fuses, about 120,000 lira. OK ?" said the mechanic.

I whistled quietly through my teeth, thinking were we about to get ripped off. Stokie paused, stepped down below to his cabin, retrieved his calculator and punched in the numbers. Turning to Scouse and I, he said, "Not as bad as it sounds, that's about £55."

He turned to the mechanic and said "Yes, that's OK. Please do it."

The mechanic looked over his shoulder up to him from his kneeling position over the morse gear on the cockpit floor and said "No problem. Go get some food for a while, OK ?"

Which was his polite code for "please clear off as I need to work in different places and you're going to get in my way."

We needed no further bidding.

"Will do, no problem !" said Stokie with a grin and we filed off Kezia onto the quayside and headed towards the boatyard gates. "That's a good result!" said Scouse. We were all smiles because it seemed that we had snatched victory from defeat yet again. The sun was shining and we were walking towards a beach front, with all the cares of a long and difficult day fading behind us.

In time-honoured fashion, Stokie failed to treat us to the slap-up lunch and beers that we felt we deserved. However, he did treat us both to an excellent and truly memorable Sicilian ice cream in a cone so there was some recompense for our lost lunch.

We walked along the beachfront of Mondello, festooned with brightly coloured parasols, casting their shade on smart sun loungers, resting on golden sand. The town had the genteel, slightly-faded atmosphere of an English regency seaside town and I felt self-conscious walking amongst holidaymakers in my battered chef's trousers and grubby t-shirt. This was another world and we did not fit in here at all. I made a silent wish to return here one day in better circumstances.

We killed three hours in total, wandering around the town in an effort to give our mechanic the time and space to work and headed back to the harbour by 5pm. We walked straight into the workshop office and found our man behind his desk, filling out paperwork which turned out to be ours.

"Ah !" he exclaimed as he saw us, finally cracking a smile. "All good, all fixed."

There were smiles all around and joint relief. We could get going and finish this "fated" journey.

"But one problem."

"Was much more expensive – you had a big short-circuit, lots of damage. Had to find new battery for Volvo Penta. Was special Marine and expensive. Had to replace alternator and some special fuses and some wiring was burned. Broken."

All this made sense to me and fitted with what I had seen of Kezia over several weeks, especially after the fire, so I wasn't surprised.

"Yes." the mechanic resumed, "so was 462,000 lira." He looked directly at Stokie, straight in the eyes, no trace of emotion. As far as he was concerned, it was a simple statement of fact.

I looked intently at Stokie and all colour had drained from his face.

"Can I use your calculator ?" he said, pointing to the mechanic, who nodded. Stokie tapped in the numbers and the exchange rate (2,200) in frantically. He had to do this three times before he was prepared to believe the damage.

"Fuck, fuck, fuck. That's 210 quid." he sighed, looking up desperately to the office ceiling.

I felt nothing at this time, neither emotionally involved or particularly interested. If anything, I was quietly siding with the mechanic. The price seemed about right for all that work and replacement of parts.

Stokie was slowly recovering himself and reaching for counter-arguments now.

"But you said 120,000 - this is about 4 times that!" holding up four fingers at the mechanic to emphasise his point.

The mechanic was unmoved. "Yes, but you were not here. Work had to be done, all had to be done - is good price. Is very good price."

Stokie now looked desperate and I was not understanding why. He was looking to me, to Scouse, the mechanic and back around us, as if we could rescue him or find a counter-argument. I was still as unmoved as the mechanic. The boat was a wreck and we had known that in Tortola. This was not my boat. Someone else owned it and we were just delivering it. Someone needed to pay the bill and it was not going to be me.

Stokie played his last, feeble card. "But I simply haven't got 462,000 lira !" he pleaded, "I just haven't got that sort of money !"

"Scouse, what cash have you got left ?"

"Twenty quid."

"Rob ?"

"Thirty-five quid. What have you got ? I know you had a kitty for the trip…"

"I'm down to a hundred and ten quid, that's all I've got left now."

Previously, I was irked by the penny-pinching, on-a-shoestring approach to the trip. Now, I was now starting to worry.

"So, how were you going to fly us back home with no money then, Stokie ?"

"That's nothing to do with it !" he snapped back. "David will book and pay for the flights when we get there, we just pick 'em up from the ticket desk at the airport. BUT we have to get there first. That's the deal."

He turned back to the mechanic. "Look, we have a hundred and sixty-five pounds in English money - can you take that ?"

The mechanic retrieved his calculator from the end of the desk. "What is exchange rate ?"

"Two thousand, two hundred" Stokie replied. More keys were pressed in response.

"No. Is not enough, I had to buy battery. Look my friend, you are taking this yacht to Greece, yes ? Why don't you make phone call to owner and get money ?" he said.

"That will take too long." said Stokie. "Can we send the money back to you in two weeks' time instead ?"

The mechanic now bridled as if he had been insulted.

"You think I'm stupid, crazy ?" he snapped at Stokie. With a theatrical sweep of his hand, he scooped up Kezia's ignition key that was lying on the desk, stood up and hung it on an empty hook along with many other keys hanging in lines on a grimy, wall-mounted board.

"When you pay, you can leave !" and waved his hand dismissively at us. Our audience was over.

Despondently, we trudged out of his office and headed back across the quayside towards Kezia. Once outside the chain link fence and out of earshot of the mechanic, Stokie stopped abruptly and turned on Scouse and I. "What the hell were we going to do now ?" he pleaded, eyes flaring.

"What about ringing David, as our man said ?" Scouse said.

"It's got to be worth a shot." said Stokie resignedly, turning on his heel and heading back towards the boatyard entrance. "Could be a while." he called over his shoulder.

Scouse and I headed back to the yacht and in time-honoured English marine tradition, in times of great stress and danger, we put the kettle on for tea. Time passed and we watched in quiet alarm, as the mechanic emerged from his office and closed the large workshop shutter by pressing an electric button located on the door frame. Once the shutter was fully down to the ground, he turned its key and removed it. He then walked to its perimeter fence, drew the two large gates shut and then fed a large chain through both halves and secured it with a padlock. He pocketed the key and headed out of the open dockyard gate, a hundred yards away, towards a small cafe still further down the road to the beachfront. His working day was done, he was gone and without an engine ignition key, we were still as marooned in Mondello as we were at midday.

Some while later, Stokie reappeared. He had recovered his temper and equilibrium but had no definitive answer.

"So what did David say then ?" I asked urgently.

"It's the weekend so no banks are open. He could wire us some money to a bank but we'll have to tell him what bank and what branch, it will take a few days. Then we have to pick it up, cash it and pay the bill. But I've got no effing clue what bank or how to go about it. My Italian goes about as far as 'due birre per favore' - two beers, please."

He sat there thoughtfully and then continued: "I'm sick to the back teeth of this guy. He gives us one price and then charges us another. It's gonna take us days to get out of here at this rate."

I was stumped and had nothing to offer. "So what do you think we should do then ?" I asked. "No idea." he replied dejectedly. "No fucking idea."

We had our usual (and unusually, even more miserable) dinner of curried mince beef and rice as our evening meal and sat there in the beautiful Sicilian evening, as the light began to fade.

Each was lost in his own thoughts and mine were becoming increasingly troubled. As I mulled over everything that had happened over the last few days and what the engineer had said, I couldn't help but feel that something was very amiss. It was

178

entirely feasible that the fire had done that much damage to the electrics but why had the engine continued to work for three days afterwards before breaking down?

Without a word, I rose from my seat in the cockpit, walked over to the steps down into the galley and climbed down. I crossed the saloon to the dining table which was actually the housing for the diesel engine, with a split, polished teak top that disguised its true function very well. Reaching down on each side of the housing, in turn, I unclipped two large chrome hooks and pried the table top apart, folding the two fibreglass halves outwards to expose the diesel engine.

This immediately attracted the attention of Stokie who had stepped up to the doorway above me.

"What you up to, Rob ? Something wrong ?" he asked.

"Leave it with me, mate", I replied over my shoulder. "I want to check something."

I surveyed the engine block and sure enough, there was a single, bright-grey, polished new part that stood out from the rest which were all covered with a thin layer of black oily soot. As I had expected, the new alternator was in place.

I closed the two halves of the engine cowling back together and clicked its hooks back together on either side and stepped back to the doorway. Instead of climbing back up the cockpit, I paused and reached out to another two hooks on either side of the cabin steps, unclipped them and pulled the ladder away and leaned it up against the engine behind me. Crouching down, I removed the burnt plywood covering to the fuse box and set it aside. Scanning the rows of fuses, I quickly confirmed that all were in place but I was mildly surprised to see that there was no gleaming replacement (or several replacements) staring back at me. The board looked untouched and I was certain that nothing had been disturbed in any way. There was no sign of any new wiring.

Wordlessly, I replaced the fuseboard cover, slotted the cabin steps back into place and climbed back up the cockpit, Stokie stepping aside to let me pass.

Next, I moved to the lid of the cockpit locker on the left, immediately above the morse lever that had been replaced in the Azores, unlocked it and lifted it. Deep in the recess below, was the main battery that I was seeking. I could see an Exide sticker with its dark blue logo and turquoise lettering between the two poles of the battery and was reassured to see it gleaming and apparently new.

Stokie was looming over me as I crouched, peering down into the locker.

"What do you see ?" he asked.

"Not sure." I replied. "Can you get me a torch ?"

He squeezed past me and disappeared down into his aft cabin, re-emerging a few seconds later with a small black torch that he handed to me. I clicked it on and again, bent over the locker and shone the beam down onto the battery.

"Bloody. Hell." I said slowly and emphatically.

"What ? What ?" exclaimed Stokie impatiently. "What's going on ?"

"Come here and look !" I instructed. He came around and crouched next to me, now peering down at the battery, illuminated by the beam of the torch.

"See here." I said. "At first glance, it looks like a brand-new battery, all clean and shiny. Happens to be an Exide just like ours was but it's a worldwide best-seller, so no real surprise there. But if you look down here..."

I shone the beam slowly around the sides of the battery which were clearly covered in dirt and grease.

"You can see it's still the same battery but the bastard has carefully cleaned and polished the top and the sticker to make it look brand new.... but the dirt gives it away. He didn't change it all. Do you see it?"

"I see it." said Stokie.

"So... he just told us that he'd had to replace the alternator, fuses, burned wiring and buy an expensive marine battery but what actually happened is that the alternator had packed up so he just fitted a new one, charged up our battery, polished it nicely and then he's trying to charge us 462,000 lira for the privilege. I thought things didn't add up."

"Didn't add up ?" Stokie exploded. "The bastard's ripping us off !" he shouted.

He paused for a second.

"But what should it have costed then ?"

"For a new alternator and a battery charge, the 55,000 lira he quoted first of all would have been about right."

"Bastard !" he exploded again.

"Fellahs." Scouse interjected. "We're not in a happy place. If the bloke was still around, we could go over there and have it out with him but he's buggered off for the day."

"Worse than that, he might not even come back in tomorrow and then we'll have to wait to have the argument with him." replied Stokie.

After several more expletives and pointless cursing of the mechanic, we slumped back into our seats in the cockpit, in brooding silence, at a loss for words to say or what to do next. In this way, we sat for over an hour, hardly speaking, thoroughly despondent.

"Sod it. Let's take our boat back." said Scouse suddenly.

"What the hell ?" I said, now truly alarmed.

"Yep, let's get the ignition key and motor on out of here." he said firmly. "Who's going to stop us then ?"

"Well, after we've done breaking and entering, taken the keys and run away with the boat, someone spots us and calls the Police, that would be an Italian marine patrol." said Stokie, with a dangerous glint in his eye.

"Whoa, no guys !" I exclaimed. "This is way out of my league" I pleaded.

"Well, you're welcome to stay and explain everything after we've gone, Rob !"

My heart was in my mouth and I felt that I was being drawn inexorably into a plot which would end with us all languishing in a Sicilian jail.

"Look, why don't we wait for him to come back in tomorrow morning, tell him that we've found him out and negotiate the right price with him ?"

"No." said Stokie firmly. "This guy has tried to rip us off. You've proved that he only did a small part of the work that he claimed he had. That's fraud."

"I'm 100% sure what we need to do now.. I have a plan." he continued. "We know where where the keys are. We get into the office, leave him exactly the cash that we agreed to at the start, grab the keys, get it done quietly. Start the engine, slip out of here and bugger off before anyone realises we've gone."

Scouse nodded.

"Rob, if we do it your way, it could take days and days and we might not even win. He's holding us to ransom. I've had enough. I just want to get home now. I say let's do it. Tonight."

"Yep, I feel the same way." said Stokie looking searchingly at me. I had no answer and felt hopeless and cornered.

"Are we all in then ?" Scouse asked us but he was looking only at me.

I sat there quietly and weighed the pros and cons and said nothing for a while. At last, I raised my head in the gathering darkness of the saloon and said in quiet resignation "OK, let's do it."

"Great !" said Scouse. "I think we need to wait until the town quietens down first. Hop the fence, break the side window to the office, grab the key and then back out."

I said nothing, knowing that to say anything ran the risk of being 'volunteered' for some part of the venture.

"And Rob, sorry to say it but you showed in Quarteira that you were the best man for scaling a 12-foot chain link fence."

Damn, I had known this was coming.

"I know nothing about how to break a window quietly." I replied.

"Neither do we." said Stokie. "But I'd say take a towel and a winch handle. Use the towel to muffle the noise, break a pane, undo the window, climb in and grab the key."

Stokie could see that I was still reluctant and gave me a reassuring smile.

"Look, I can see you're not happy with this. None of us are. But the way I see it, we'll be doing the right thing. We agreed to pay £55 so let's leave that with him. And if we get caught, it'll make things look a whole lot better."

"Yep. You're absolutely right. I'm in." I smiled weakly.

Just after 23:30hrs, the three of us were lined up outside the padlocked perimeter fence to the workshop. Scouse had a small towel in one hand and a winch handle in the other. We were all staring intently towards the corner of the workshop where we knew the office to be. I was scanning the open dockyard gate beyond that and the road to the small cafe several hundred yards down, where we last saw our mechanic heading. We hadn't seen him leave the cafe but equally, we had not been watching and many hours had passed since he left work.

Stokie handed me the £55 cash in notes which I stuffed into the front pocket of my shorts.

Turning to my task, there was too much light for my liking. Sodium streetlamps bathed the outside of the main dockyard fence in their orange glow. There were more lights lining the road to the cafe and beyond, right down to the beachfront and Mondello town itself.

On a more positive note, there were no lights showing inside the dockyard, apart from the small knee-high lamps that were dotted around the pontoons to help sailors get off or onto their boats. There were only three other yachts around us and we knew that they were unoccupied. Most importantly, there were no guard dogs either. It was time for action.

As I had rashly demonstrated in Quarteira, I reached up and grabbed the fence above my head and started to climb the 12-foot fence in a coordinated fashion using the chain links as both hand and foot-holds. Within seconds, I was straddling the top and repeated the exercise down the other side. When I reached the ground, Scouse fed the towel through the fence to me and then passed the handle through with much greater care. Words were unnecessary. We understood that if either of us dropped the metal handle, its metallic clang would ring clearly across the whole dockyard and beyond.

I could feel my adrenaline rising but I tried to ignore it. I was committed now. I turned further to the right and struck a line towards the other end of the workshop and I was quickly out of the light and into the welcome shadows. Once I reached the end of the building, I padded quietly along the front of the building to the other corner and peered around it.

I didn't like this. There was not much light on the short side of the workshop where I needed to break the window but it was the closest to the dockyard entrancmorend most exposed. Nevertheless, I slipped around the corner and looked up. I could clearly see the old cast-iron window handle on the other side of a single pane of glass - my target. I folded the towel over itself neatly to create a pad, held it to the window and hit it with the business end of the winch gently but firmly. I heard a crack but the glass pane held. I pulled back the pad to inspect my work, replaced it and then made a slightly harder blow. The pane still held. Again, I checked my work, replaced the pad and struck again, still harder. This time, the glass gave way with hardly any sound, that was until the tinkling fragments of broken glass hit the concrete floor in the office. I looked around in some alarm for a few seconds but there was no reaction and no movement outside the dockyard. No-one had heard. I reached gingerly through the broken pane and moved the window handle up. I pulled gently on the edge of the frame and the window swung open towards me easily. I withdrew my hand, grasped the window ledge and pulled myself up and onto it. I stepped down heavily into the office and straightened up. I looked to the board of keys and was relieved to see Kezia's ignition key still where the mechanic left it, gleaming slightly in the reflected light from outside. I pocketed it carefully. Next, I drew the wad of sterling notes from my trouser pocket and arranged them neatly in the middle of a blotter of the engineer's desk, so they were clearly visible. Finally, I levered myself back up onto the window ledge, then dropped down on the outside again. In a fit of tidiness, I closed the window back enough to fool a casual observer doing a visual check of the building - who knows, it might buy us time later?

Now, more urgently, feeling very exposed as the deed was now done, I picked up the towel and winch, retraced my steps along the front of the workshop and made a beeline back to my original entry point at the fence where Stokie and Scouse were still outlined in the darkness.

"You got it ?" hissed Stokie. "Yes !" I hissed back. "Here take these !" and threaded the winch and towel carefully back through the fence. I scaled the chain-link in exactly the same way as I had before, fueled by adrenalin.

We crept back to the yacht and assembled in the cockpit.

"Very well done, mate !" murmured Stokie to me as I pulled the ignition key from my pocket and handed it to him. "Bloody great !" agreed Scouse. "We hardly heard a sound, you did great !"

"Thanks !" I said. "I was bricking it but I think we're OK. How were we going do this Stokie ? We need to get going quick !" I didn't want to get nabbed at this stage after everything I'd been through.

"I've thought it through. We'll go right now. You two loosen the lines so you're ready to go. I'll make sure the engine starts then you take the lines off immediately, jump on and we go."

We did exactly that. Scouse slipped over the stern, untied the line from the mooring cleat on the dock and I did the same on the port side where the boat was touching. We both hissed "Ready !" back to Stokie at the helm, in turn. And now for the moment of truth. Stokie turned the ignition key and a high-pitched tone rang out to tell us that the engine was ready to start. I was anxious at the sound yet felt relieved at the same time. With a further turn of the key, the diesel engine started noisily, echoing across the quiet quayside and across the boatyard.

"GO ! GO !" urged Stokie. Scouse and I grabbed our respective coils of rope and leapt onto the boat simultaneously. To Stokie's credit, without over-revving the engine, he slipped it into forward gear as if we were making a normal exit and we cruised out of our mooring and headed towards the harbour entrance. Whilst he looked forward and steered, Scouse and I looked intently back over the stern, watching for any sign that we'd been spotted.

There was none. The boatyard remained exactly as before, in semi-darkness, ringed only by the perimeter lights. Nothing was moving. We reached the red navigation light on the end of the harbour wall and pointed out towards the open water. I cursed the clatter of our diesel engine, still reverberating out across the docks.

"Looks like we got away with it !" Stokie exclaimed, exultant. I was excited that we had pulled off a daring stunt against the odds and sat in the cockpit with a broad, beaming smile.

My smiled faded in an instant. Still vigilant, I was looking back towards the quayside and watched with horror as four figures came running into the dockyard at speed, silhouetted under the lights. They ran up to the berth where Kezia was moored, stopped abruptly and looked out directly towards us as we cleared the harbour wall.

"Fermare !"

"Torna qui !"

We didn't speak Italian but we had been found out and we were in trouble. One of the voices was clearly our mechanic and he didn't sound particularly happy.

Stokie gunned the throttle, not to full power but the revs rose dramatically and the yacht surged forward with newfound power. "God, I hope the engine holds out." I thought to myself, given that we had only just had it repaired. It could be our only salvation now.

"Christ, I think they might be launching a boat." shouted Scouse in disbelief.

Sure enough, the men had turned their attention away from us, had opened the double gate in the chain-link fence that I had just scaled and were running towards the workshop's shutter. My last glimpse of the building was of the shutter opening and the workshop lights being switched on, brilliantly illuminating the small harbour in an instant.

Well clear of the harbour entrance by now, Stokie swung the wheel and steered us due eastwards, towards Messina.

Scouse and I continued to crane our necks back towards the receding harbour entrance. For several minutes, nothing changed and we continued to put distance between us and Mondello. Silently, Stokie reached down and switched on our navigation lights and I looked over at him quizzically. "Yeah, I get it." he said to me, "but it's so damned busy out here tonight, other people need to see us." Given that there were no signs of pursuit, I nodded and turned back to keeping watch over the stern towards the town. Fishing trawlers, container vessels and a cruise line were threading around the shipping lane that we were about to join and all of them were bigger than us.

At around 01:00hrs, Scouse still seated on the other side of the stern from me, said out loud, "I think I can hear an outboard". I scrambled to look back and sure enough in the far distance, I could see a green light to the left and a red light immediately to its right. And I could hear the higher-pitched whine of an outboard behind us.

"Don't panic." said Stokie. "We need to be sure they are following us. Let's find out!' and he swung the wheel twenty degrees northwards and set on a new course. It took a further three minutes to confirm it but the lights had turned too - a powerful dinghy was hunting us!

We had no illusions that its occupants would be looking to bargain over the price of the job when they caught up with us.

"Time for Plan B." shouted Stokie. He turned back towards our easterly course and held there, which seemed madness to me, with our navigation lights still shining brightly but he would not be persuaded otherwise. He gripped the wheel with tight determination, occasionally glancing behind the boat to measure the distance that the dinghy had gained on us. Getting a sound beating or worse from some Sicilian gentlemen (and those from Palermo especially) did not seem like a sound "Plan B" to me, at this moment.

Suddenly, after three minutes of this, with our pursuers drawing inexorably closer, Stokie reached down, flicked off the navigation lights and plunged the yacht into darkness. He swung the wheel 90 degrees to north and held this new course for three minutes which he measured by getting me to count out the time, lacking a wristwatch still. On the count, he then swung the yacht another 20 degrees westwards and got me to count out another ten minutes. Meanwhile, Scouse and I were still watching the dinghy's lights and listening keenly for its engine. It seemed to have drawn level with our position but on a different course. Stokie said nothing and stared grimly forward.

Another ten minutes later, we had steered 45 degrees east, followed by a further 45 degree turn eastwards, for another ten minute period. And so, after a series of apparently-random navigation legs, we found ourselves at first light off Cape Milazzo, some twenty miles west from the top of the Messina Straits between Sicily and Italy.

More importantly, there was no trace of our pursuers. We had finally and decisively shaken them off. We did not celebrate and we were not jubilant. We felt that we had been at war all night, none of us had had any sleep and there was a strong feeling of "There but for the grace of God go I." It didn't bear thinking about what would have happened if they had caught up with us.

Chapter Ten

Groovy Gouvia

As we turned the most north-easterly cape of Sicily, Torre Faro, into the Strait of Messina, Stokie briefed us on what we were about to face.

"You need to be on your toes, guys." he said grimly.

"Firstly, the current is vicious. Think of it like a funnel, channelling all the water down from the Med and squeezing it between Sicily and Italy, so watch out for that."

"Next, you're never going to see as many ferries crossing both ways - it's worse than the Channel, so look out for anyone trying to run us down. You might think 'steam gives way to sail' but those rules don't seem to apply here."

"Finally, we've got a following wind behind us, so with the current, we're going to be going like the clappers. Wits about you."

And with that, we were off.

In seconds, I could feel Kezia surging forward on what was only a few knots of current but this added to the following 15 knot wind. She seemed to be flying faster than at any other time on our voyage. We sailed three miles south-west, rounding the headland, where the channel was only 2 miles across. Suddenly, the straits widened in front of us, the boat turned directly south and we could see the long coastlines of Calabria and Sicily, left and right of us, gleaming in the brilliant sunshine.

The surface of the water rippled with the strong wind across it and there were whitecaps everywhere.

Our mainsail and Genoa jib were full to bursting and pulled us along at great speed, straight as an arrow towards our exit point and the Ionian Sea, some 25 miles away.

Having adjusted quickly to the new sailing conditions, we were immediately faced with the main danger that Stokie had warned us about - ferries.

Large white ships carrying both passengers and cars were vying between Villa San Giovanni on the mainland to our left and the

Port of Messina in Sicily to our right. But the problem was that they were crossing both ways and we were trespassing in their dominion. It was my job on the port side to watch and shout out all shipping movements from the east and Scouse had to watch the west. Through a series of deft course changes, Stokie threaded us between them. At no point did we feel that we were about to be run down but those were tense moments.

Soon, we were beyond the ferries' routes and the normal sailing tempo resumed, albeit still travelling at this heightened speed. Mount Etna came into sight, far to the south-west, with its summit wreathed in clouds, as ominous and foreboding as Mount Doom in Lord of the Rings.

We sailed on until we approached a point equidistant between Messina and Reggio Calabria on the Italian coast and then all hell broke loose.

There were ferries crossing between these cities but these were no normal ships. These were hydrofoils! These gleaming white vessels started the first miles of their journey settled in the water like any other ferry. However, once clear of their ports, they accelerated dramatically and rose up out of the water on their hydrofoils, with their bows pointing skywards which reduced drag and increased their speed.

So, where previously we were having to track ferries running both ways, at 10 knots across the Straits, Scouse and I now had to anticipate the movements of new traffic running at three times the speed. Even worse, they seemed blind to other vessels and charged as straight as arrows in flight, implacably, with no sign of adjusting their courses at any point. The sledges on which they sat threw vast plumes of water into the air which created turbulent wakes that took ages to settle after they had passed. Again, with Scouse and I shouting what we were seeing back to Stokie, he navigated another safe course through them and we emerged on the south side, both shaken and stirred like badly-made Martinis.

We sailed on for another three hours, adjusting our course to 150 degrees as the coast of Calabria rounded slightly to the east but the Strait of Messina was not quite done with us yet. The northerly wind accelerated to 35 knots and caught us unawares. With a sharp crack, the Genoa sail wrapped around the forestay, the wire cable that ran from the top of the mast to the tip of the bow and then started to flap perilously. It then proceeded to continue wrapping around the stay and itself, turning quickly into a shapeless, angry and noisy mess.

"Rob, take the helm !" shouted Stokie and he leapt forward towards the bow, as I grabbed the wheel. He seized Scouse by the sleeve as he ran forwards and within seconds, had his arms around the sail, trying to protect it from itself.

"Rob, 180 degrees due south and do not wander off." he barked at me over his shoulder. He was trying to keep the wind directly behind us and minimise the stresses on the sail which was threatening to tear itself apart.

So, I kept rigidly to this new course. It took them ages to release the sail and untangle it. When the sail was no longer at risk, they worked methodically together to unpick the folds and twists and I watched from the wheel, my attention no longer focused on other ships and boats.

They made very slow progress, so badly wrapped was the sail. As Stokie and Scouse laboured, I steered Kezia southwards in a straight line, unable to follow the Italian coastline as we had originally intended but out into the wide Ionian Sea.

Some two hours later, we rounded the heel of Italy and were able to set course for Corfu. The wind had come around to the east and dropped to less than 5 knots. The sky had clouded over completely and the contrast seemed incredible to me, after the exhilarating, windy and bright day that we had left behind us.

PLAYING CARDS IN A HURRICANE

Day 71 - Wednesday 18th May 1983, 06:00hrs

On a course of 65°, we were now heading in a straight-line for journey's end, Corfu.

We spent much of this day "motor sailing", using the engine to drive us forward but with the jib sail giving us extra power. It was a strange combination as I could feel the engine driving the yacht forward, conducting its power up to the boat wheel in my hands and at the same time, the sail was pulling us forward.

But the wind was a fickle friend today. It picked up, our sails filled and just at the moment when I felt that the engine was no longer needed, the wind dropped back again. So with plenty of diesel on board in our sprint for the finish line, I kept the engine going and when the wind gusted for a few minutes, I merely knocked it into neutral, knowing that it wouldn't last and I would need to put it into gear soon.

In this way, the day passed and our chatter was bright, eager and optimistic. This would be our last full day at sea and we had only 90 miles left. There would be no "hell or high water" now.

Day 72 - Thursday 19th May 1983, 06:00hrs

By dawn, the wind was picking up and visibility was improving. As I came out on deck to a blazing hot sun, I looked to the east and saw two islands on the far horizon.

"What are those islands ?" I asked Scouse.

He was slouched back on his cockpit seat, with one arm lazily on the wheel, as this was easy sailing. He had been on watch since 04:00hrs and I reckoned that he was thinking of his bed.

"No idea. Could be Greek, hope it's not communist Albania. They'll catch us and throw us in jail for trespass."

I opened Stokie's hatch and peered down into the fetid darkness. We rarely intruded into the Captain's quarters – perhaps it was a maritime tradition of a ratings respect for rank. Or perhaps it was the rank smell.

"Hey Stokie." I called quietly. "When do you expect to hit Corfu ?".

Wordlessly, he bounded out of bed gracefully – well as gracefully as a weathered, half-asleep, unwashed and unshaven skipper could manage at this hour. He pushed past me and stood with his feet apart, shielding his eyes as he looked to the East.

"Just about now m'boy." He turned to me with a broad smile. "Just about now !"

Within three hours, we were coursing down the western coast of Corfu. We were no longer motoring and the wind was so strong that we had to put a reef in the mainsail. Mother Nature seemed intent on giving us a send-off to remember and the strong tidal current caused Kezia to accelerate even faster. Not exactly the drama of the Straits of Messina a couple of days previously but very close. We rushed past the southern tip of Corfu and instead of turning north towards our destination, Stokie pointed us eastwards towards mainland Greece, which was appearing through the early morning heat haze in front of us.

"Hey what you up to ?" Scouse exclaimed as if his captain had suddenly lost all sense of direction. "Corfu is thataway !" and pointed northwards.

"Yeah, I know that, fathead. They don't have any immigration there so we have to go and check in on the mainland first."

"You might have told us !" he said deflated.

Scouse and I looked at each other despondently. Clearly journey's end had just been postponed by a few more hours. To wile away the time, I decided to spruce myself up and headed down into the saloon. I poured hot water into the galley sink and proceeded to shave off my thick beard.

It took quite a while. The razor was so overwhelmed that I had to stop. After three months at sea, my beard seemed to have become quite attached to me and was putting up a decent resistance. I found a pair of scissors from the first-aid kit and cut most of it away. Even then, every subsequent swipe of the razor gathered a clump of hair that had to be removed from the blades before I could take the next one but finally, the job was done. I was clean-shaven and my face glistened healthily.

Sometime later, I emerged on deck and to my great surprise, my esteemed colleagues fell about the deck in gales of laughter. I was confused but gathered that I had caused the hilarity, mainly because they were both pointing at me in disbelief.

"Hey Scouse, whaddya make of that ?"

"Quick call the police ! Someone has kidnapped Rob and replaced him with some white-chinned bastard instead !"

Then it dawned on me that shaving off my beard in the last few hours of a "grande voyage" was a very poor idea. I was deeply sun-tanned, lean and healthy after weeks on the ocean.

And I now had a very white, gleaming chin to go home with.

We arrived at the port of Igoumenitsa on the Greek mainland and moored up just in time to see the customs officials leaving their building *en masse,* lock up and disappear for a long lunch. Standing on the concrete dockside, we amused ourselves by taking a few last photos in the incinerating summer heat. There was no shade so we waited happily because we knew the end was nigh. Eventually, the officers returned, our passports and yacht papers were checked and stamped and we were free to sail on to Corfu. We were in Greece - finally.

At 15:00hrs, we motored back westwards towards Corfu and I took the helm for the last time.

The sea had flattened to a mirror and it was a beautiful sight, as we headed towards the greenery of Corfu in the distance. Suddenly, a swordfish broke surface and jumped high out of the water near to our starboard side and we gasped in wonder. For a few short seconds, it's 10' length was framed in mid-air, water streaming from its sword and flanks before it crashed back into the water and disappeared .

"That was one heck of a farewell salute !" said Scouse, beaming.

At 18:30hrs, we motored into the marina at Gouvia as if it was any other port that we had called into – or more probably been towed into – along our route.

We were triumphant. Considering the dangers that we had faced and the difficulties we had overcome, it would not have been out of place to see the town's brass band heralding our arrival and locals throwing garlands of flowers onto Kezia's deck after her herculean achievement of crossing 4,038 miles of wild ocean.

Instead, yachtsman, local boatmen and tourists paused to watch this small battered white yacht coast smoothly up to a pontoon and moor up with military precision. They saw three shabbily-dressed and ill-kempt men that were completely out of place in this beautiful island port. Clearly, there was a story behind the arrival of this unremarkable boat. They watched the men disembark and shake hands enthusiastically and warmly, almost as if they were celebrating something. Within minutes, the men were lost from sight as they walked along the wooden pontoon into the heart of Gouvia, no doubt in search of an ice-cold beer in the evening heat, just like any other tourists.

My final entry in the logbook read:

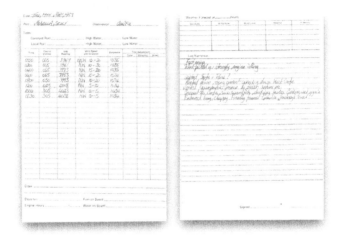

Chapter Eleven

Afterword

I returned home with a renewed sense of direction and resolve, determined not to waste any more time. I enrolled in college on a Computer Science course and became a software developer. Whilst never my first choice, this has given me an interesting and rewarding career lasting 30 years. It took me from the City of London, to eastern Europe immediately after the fall of the Berlin Wall, to the States, to Singapore, Australia and Asia for 7 years and thence, back to the UK. I married my college sweetheart and we had three wonderful, talented children. We parted after 25 years and I moved back to the beautiful Malvern Hills in Worcestershire. Nowadays, I live in Bristol with Kate who has been my inspiration and support to finally finish this book.

I never had a desire to make a career from my yacht delivery experience. As someone once said, "sailing is days of unmitigated boredom, punctuated by moments of terror." A sailor has to be lucky every day. After the trip, I slowly lost contact with Stokie and Scouse although we met up for the next three years at the annual Earls Court Boat Show, to drink Guinness together and celebrate our achievement.

Many young people are drawn to travel to gather new experiences and test themselves. In the old days, young men were told to "Join the Army. It will make a man of you". The three months that I spent on Kezia certainly tested and changed me for the better. I was pleased to find that in moments of danger, I could still function and obey orders. Those tough experiences helped to forge my character in a way that I have been able to draw upon ever since, giving me an inner strength and resilience in my worst times. When the chips are down, I have been able to say to myself "how does this actually compare to sitting next to a life raft, waiting to abandon ship ?"

I have a life-long legacy of that trip to this day. I am often reminded of one particular night and how I felt at the time. Whenever I'm home, late at night, and the rain is falling heavily and stormy winds are buffeting the house, I am transported back to a darkened attic room in Porto Velho, looking out gratefully over a harbour, saying to myself "Thank God I am here, safe and dry and not out there in a hurricane".

THE END

Made in the USA
Monee, IL
17 February 2023